A Will is

in Virginia

2nd Edition

SIMPLE, PRACTICAL THINGS
A VIRGINIA RESIDENT CAN DO TO

- ❖ PRESERVE ASSETS
- ❖ AVOID PROBATE
- ❖ AVOID GUARDIANSHIP
- ❖ PROVIDE FOR HEALTH CARE
- ❖ PROVIDE FOR THE FAMILY'S CARE

By AMELIA E. POHL, ESQ.
and
Virginia Attorney
STEPHEN J. KAUFMANN

EAGLE PUBLISHING COMPANY OF BOCA

The purpose of this book is to provide the reader with an informative overview of the subject; but laws change frequently and are subject to different interpretations as courts rule on the meaning or effect of a law. This book is sold with the under-standing that neither the authors, nor the editors, nor the publisher, nor the distributors of this book are engaging in, or rendering, legal, accounting, financial planning, medical, or any other professional service. If you need legal, accounting, medical, financial planning or any other expert advice, you should seek the services of a licensed professional.

This book is intended for use by the consumer for his or her own benefit. If you use this book to counsel someone about the law or tax matters, then that may be considered to be an unauthorized and illegal practice.

WEB SITES: Web sites appear throughout the book. These Web sites are offered for the convenience of the reader only. Publication of these Web site addresses is not an endorsement by the authors, editors or publishers of this book.

EAGLE PUBLISHING COMPANY OF BOCA
4199 N. Dixie Highway, #2
Boca Raton, FL   33431   E-mail: info@eaglepublishing.com

Printed in the United States of America
ISBN 1-932464-07-7
Library of Congress Catalog Card Number 2002100529

ii

A Will is Not Enough in Virginia
2nd Edition

CONTENTS

Introduction

Over the years, as we practiced law, we noticed that the questions people have about Wills, Trusts, powers of attorney, avoiding probate and guardianship, preserving assets, providing health care for themselves and their families, are much the same client to client. Many people are concerned about who will control their finances should they become too aged or too ill to do so themselves. Of even more concern is their health care:

Who will make my medical decisions if I can't do so myself?

How can I pay for my health care?

How much and what type of insurance should I have?

How can I avoid guardianship?

Others worry about the care of family members. Those with minor children worry:

Who will care for my minor child if I become incapacitated or die?

Is there a way to make sure my child has enough money to see him through college?

Those with elderly parents worry:

How can I manage my parent's finances should my parent become too aged or ill to do so?

Can my parent qualify for MEDICAID?

If my parent dies, will I need to go through Probate?

Is there a way to avoid Probate?

We agreed that a book answering such questions would be of service to the general public. We wish to thank all of the clients, whom we have had the honor and pleasure to serve, for providing us with the impetus to write this book.

Stephen J. Kaufmann

STEPHEN J. KAUFMANN is noted nationally for his dedication to helping people protect their assets, privacy and quality of life as an Elder Law and Estate Planning attorney. He has over 30 years experience in Elder Law and Estate Planning and is the former Deputy Commissioner of Insurance, Virginia State Corporation Commission. Mr. Kaufmann is an educator and nationally known author of many estate planning books and educational courses in the Legal-Financial Estate Planning and Insurance industry. He has been noted in Newsweek, published in Financial Planning, US News and World Report, Life Association News (LAN-Now Advisor), Life Insurance Selling, Broker World and appears often in national publications.

Steve practices through his law firm - ABC LAW, and serves families, farm and small business owners throughout Virginia and works with other attorneys, financial, insurance and other professionals and their clients nationally. He is a humorous and educational public speaker for many local and national conferences.

Steve presents programs on radio, television, and national educational forums. He has spoken before U.S. Congressional and state legislative committees and was responsible for writing the laws on Long Term Care and other insurance products as the former Virginia Deputy Insurance Commissioner. He is the President and Founder of The Estate Planning Institute and the professional designation Study program, CEPP, Chartered Estate Planning Practitioner.

Steve is a member of the National Academy of Elder Law Attorneys, past president of the Central Virginia Chapter of Chartered Life Underwriters. He is also a member of the International Association of Financial Planners and former Chairperson for Federal and State Legislative Committee, Virginia Association of Insurance and Financial Advisors. He is the founder of the Kaufmann Foundation, a charitable organization that provides educational programs to the public and gifts to programs that inspire, educate and help people protect their quality of life around the world.

Steve has been in private and government practice since 1974. He graduated from Boston College (MBA) in 1970, and from Suffolk University Law School in 1974.

Steve and his wife Bonnie Kaufmann, an instructor and insurance-life style and business consultant have five sons ranging in ages from 17 to 30. They live in Luray, Virginia. Together they present the radio program "Law and Your Money©" that is aired on different radio stations. You can find the time and location of their next radio broadcast at their Web site http://lifeplanners.org

Amelia E. Pohl, Esq.

Before becoming an attorney in 1985, AMELIA E. POHL taught mathematics on both the high school and college level. During her tenure as Associate Professor of Mathematics at Prince George's Community College in Maryland, she wrote several books including:
Probability: A Set Theory Approach,
Principals of Counting
Common Stock Sense.

During her practice of law Attorney Pohl observed that many people want to reduce the high cost of legal fees by performing or assisting with their own legal transactions.

Attorney Pohl found that, with a bit of guidance, people are able to perform many legal transactions for themselves. Attorney Pohl utilizes her background as teacher, author and attorney to provide that "bit of guidance" to the general public in the form of self-help legal books that she has written. Because there is such variation in the laws from state to state, each book written by Attorney Pohl is state specific.

With the assistance of an attorney licensed to practice in the given state, Amelia Pohl is currently "translating" this book for the remaining states.

Call **EAGLE PUBLISHING COMPANY OF BOCA** at (800) 824-0823 to learn of the availability of this book for any other state.

Acknowledgment

We wish to thank Virginia attorney PAULA L. PEADEN for her review of the cited Medicaid statutes and numbers for conformity with Virginia law.

Ms. Peaden is a shareholder in the law firm of Parker, Pollard & Brown, P.C. located in Richmond, Virginia. She practices primarily in the areas of wills, estate planning, disability planning and Elder Law. Ms. Peaden served as a part-time administrative law judge for the Department of Medical Assistance Services.

Paula L. Peaden is a member of the Trust and Estate Section and past chairperson of the Board of Governors of the Elder Law Section of the Virginia State Bar. She is also a director of the Virginia Chapter of the National Academy of Elder Law Attorneys.

THE DESIGN ARTIST

LUBOSH CECH designed the cover of this book.

Lubosh Cech is the founder of OKO DESIGN STUDIO located in Portland, Oregon. He designs promotional materials for print and digital media. He has received numerous rewards for both graphic design and painting. For more information about Mr. Cech and the OKO Design Studio visit his Web site.

http://www.okodesignstudio.com

The photograph on the cover is that of the Virginia State Capitol by S. Solum/PhotoLink.

Reading the Law

Where applicable, we identified the state statute or federal statute that is the basis of the discussion. We did this as a reference, and also to encourage the general public to read the law as it is written. Prior to the Internet the only way you could look up the law was to physically take yourself to the local courthouse law library or the law section of a public library. Today all of the state and federal statutes are literally at your finger tips. They are just a mouse click away on the Internet. To look up a statute all you need is the address of the Web site and the identifying number of the statute.

 FEDERAL STATUTES
http://www4.law.cornell.edu/uscode

VIRGINIA STATUTES
http://www.state.va.us

Virginia has compiled their laws into some 66 Titles. For example INSURANCE is Title 38 (as well as 38.1 and 38.2), HEALTH is 32.1. WILLS AND DECEDENTS' ESTATES' 64.1, and so on. We will identify the statute by the number of the title and the section within that title. For example, to look up (VA 64.1-69.1) this statute, you would go to the statute section of the Web site. From there to the Table of Contents to Title 64.1 and then to Section 69.1. An easier method is to type 64.1-69.1 in the "Search" box.

You may find it both interesting and profitable to read the law as it is actually written, if you come across a topic in the book that is important to you..

When You Need A Lawyer

The purpose of the book is to give the reader a basic understanding of Estate Planning. It is not intended as a substitute for legal counsel or any other kind of professional advice. If you have any legal question, then you should to seek the counsel of an attorney. When looking for an attorney, consider three things: EXPERTISE, COST and PERSONALITY.

EXPERTISE

The state of Virginia does not have a program to certify that an attorney is specialized in a particular area of law. However, attorneys are allowed to state that they are certified by an accredited institution, if such is the case. For example, the National Elder Law Foundation has a certification program for the field of Elder Law. An attorney certified by the Foundation, or other program such as being a Chartered Estate Planning Practitioner is allowed to make that fact known to the public.

There is a Lawyer Referral Service located in each county Bar Association. They can refer you to an attorney in your area who practices the type of law that you seek. You can get the number of the Lawyer Referral Service in your county by calling the State Bar of Virginia at (800) 552-7977.

You can get information about the State Bar Referral Service at their Web site.

 VIRGINIA STATE BAR
http://www.vsb.org/

One of the most reliable ways to find an attorney is through personal referral. Ask your friends, family or business acquaintances if they used an attorney for the field of law that you seek and whether they were pleased with the results. It is important to employ an attorney who is experienced in the area of law you seek. Your friend may have a wonderful Estate Planning attorney, but if you suffered an injury to your body, then you need an attorney experienced in Personal Injury.

Before employing an attorney, ask how long he has practiced in that field of law and what percentage of his practice is devoted to that type of law.

COST

In addition to the attorney's experience, it is important to check what it will cost in attorney fees. When you call for an appointment ask what the attorney will charge for the initial consultation and the approximate cost for the service you seek. Ask whether there will be additional costs such as filing fees, accounting fees, expert witness fees, etc.

If the least expensive attorney is out of your price range then you can call your local county Bar Association for the telephone number of the Legal Aid office nearest you.

The American Bar Association has a directory of Virginia Legal Services Programs at the General Public Resources section of its Web site.

 AMERICAN BAR ASSOCIATION
http://www.abanet.org

PERSONALITY

Of equal importance to the attorney's experience and legal fees, is your relationship with the attorney. How easy was it to reach the attorney? Did you go through layers of receptionists and legal assistants before being allowed to speak to the attorney? Did the attorney promptly return your call? If you had difficulty reaching the attorney, then you can expect similar problems should you employ that attorney.

Did the attorney treat you with respect? Did the attorney treat you paternally with a "father knows best" attitude or did he treat you as an intelligent person with the ability to understand the options available to you and the ability to make your own decision based on the information provided to you?

Are you able to understand and easily communicate with the attorney? Is he speaking to you in plain English or is his explanation of the matter so full of legalese to be almost meaningless to you?

Do you find the attorney's personality to be pleasant or grating? Sometimes people rub each other the wrong way. It is like rubbing a cat the wrong way. Stroking a cat from head to tail is pleasing to the cat, but petting it in the opposite direction, no matter how well intended, causes friction. If the lawyer makes you feel annoyed or uncomfortable, then find another attorney.

It is worth the effort to take the time to interview as many attorneys as it takes to find one with the right expertise, fee schedule and personality for you.

The Organization of the Book

Many people who have a Will think they have their affairs in order, reasoning that should they die everything will go to the people named in the Will and somehow things will all be taken care of. But this is a simplistic view. There are many more things to consider.

1. What exactly will your beneficiaries inherit?
2. How will your property be transferred?
3. Can you (should you) avoid Probate?
4. Can you avoid a challenge to your Will?

The first four chapters of this book deal with these basic issues. Once you read these chapters you will have an understanding of what will happen to your property should you die, regardless of whether you do, or do not, have a Will. The rest of the book deals with things a Will <u>cannot</u> do: manage your debt, appoint someone to make your medical decisions should you be unable to do so, care for minor or disabled child, provide for your health care and apply for MEDICAID should the need arise.

GLOSSARY

This book is designed for the average reader. Legal terminology has been kept to a minimum. There is a glossary at the end of the book in case you come across a legal term that is not familiar to you.

FICTITIOUS NAMES AND EVENTS

The examples in this book are based loosely on actual events; however, all names are fictitious; and the events, as portrayed, are fictitious.

MALE GENDER USED

Rather than use he/she or himself/herself, for simplicity, we have used the male gender.

Your Financial Check-up 1

To understand why *A Will is Not Enough in Virginia* you need to know what a Will can and cannot do. One thing a Will can do is make a gift of all you own (your *Estate*). One of the things a Will cannot do is preserve and protect your property during your lifetime. For that, you need to think about risks to your property (poor investments, theft, loss through acts of nature, etc.) and what you can do to minimize or eliminate such risk. In other words, you need an *Estate Plan* for the care and management of your property during your lifetime.

The average person may protest "I don't have an Estate; none the less an Estate Plan." But you do. Everyone who has property, has an Estate Plan. You may never have verbalized your Estate Plan, or even thought about it, but it's there none-the-less. For example, take the case of the college student purchasing his first car. If his parents bankroll the purchase, the son may offer to hold the car jointly with them. The son's Estate is his car. His Estate Plan is to hold the car jointly with his parents so that they will own the car should anything happen to him.

This may not be the best Estate Plan. Holding the car jointly with his parents may make them liable for injuries or damages should the car be involved in an accident. If the young man's parents are familiar with Virginia law, they would be wise to refuse the offer and reassure their son "You can make a Will and make us the beneficiary of your car. But even if you die without a Will, we are your heirs under Virginia law. Either way we will inherit the car. Just make sure to drive carefully and carry enough car insurance."

This is a better Estate Plan. It gives the young man maximum control over his Estate (i.e., his car) during his lifetime. He can sell the car, mortgage it, or trash it, all as he sees fit. If he follows his parent's advice, of driving carefully and purchasing sufficient insurance, his Estate will have maximum protection. If he dies without a Will, and is single and without children, under Virginia's LAWS OF DESCENT AND DISTRIBUTION, his parents will inherit his Estate. And that is just the way the son wants things at this stage of his life.

Simple situation, simple Estate Plan. But, for most of us, life isn't all that simple. We may own many items of value and have loved ones who rely on us. At some point in our lives, we need to ask:

> *How can I make sure that my property will be inherited by my choice of beneficiary?*

> *How can I arrange to have my property inherited quickly and at minimum cost?*

> *How can I achieve these goals and yet have maximum control and protection of my property during my lifetime?*

We will explore the different ways to answer these questions so that you can decide on an Estate Plan that is best for you. But before doing so you need to know what property you own; i.e., how much your Estate is worth. If you are married and your spouse handles all of the finances, it may be that you have no idea of the value of your Estate.

That was the case with Kristin. She met Matt when they were both at the pinnacle of their careers, but they had no more insight into their precarious position than fireworks in a summer sky just before self-destruct.

Kristin was a model. Not the best, nor the most beautiful, but she made a comfortable living. She moved in a circle of famous models. She reflected off of their radiance, making her appear more attractive than she actually was.

Matt worked in middle management for one of those high tech companies. Like Kristin, he was not particularly gifted but he happened to be in Silicon Valley just at the time the high stakes investors were showing extraordinary, if not misguided, confidence in the industry. The good times were rolling. It never crossed Matt's mind that this would one day end. He spent the money as fast as it came in.

Kristin was impressed with the lavish gifts Matt gave to her. She, and her family, thought she made quite a catch when she announced her engagement. After the wedding she continued to model, but it took a lot of traveling and Matt resented her time away. Eventually, she agreed to stop working altogether. After all, why should she, the wife of a wealthy man, need to continue with the rigors of a model's life of diet and exercise?

Matt never told Kristin about his financial difficulties. All she knew was that he was drinking quite a bit. Her suspicion that he also was into drugs was verified when he died, suddenly, because of an overdose. Her shock and sadness turned to anger when she discovered that all he owned was mortgaged and he was heavily in debt. He even borrowed money from her family without her knowledge!

Matt's creditors took it all. The house, the boat, the Porsche, everything. If only Kristin had investigated the true state of their finances, she could have arranged to set aside the money she earned prior to her marriage and not end up as she did, a destitute widow, past her prime.

DETERMINING YOUR NET WORTH

Even if you are single you may not know the value of your Estate because you have not taken the time to actually sit down and figure it out. To get maximum benefit from this book, you need to take a few minutes to determine your *Net Worth* i.e. the current value of your Estate.

ASSETS

$_____   Cash (certificates of deposit, bank accounts, etc.)

$_____   Tangible personal property (jewelry, motor vehicles, private art, stamp or coin collections, etc.)

$_____   Cash value of insurance policies

$_____   Securities (stocks, bonds, etc.)

$_____   Cash value of pension plans, IRAs, etc.

$_____   Cash value of a partnership or other business interest

$_____   Real property (residence, time share, lot, condo, cooperatives, etc.)

$_____   TOTAL VALUE OF ASSETS

It may be that you have a loan on your car or home, or any of the above items. You need to subtract away monies you owe to get the bottom line value of what you own:

LIABILITIES

$_____   Private loans

$_____   Mortgage Balance

$_____   Credit card debt

$_____   Car loan or car lease balance

$_____   TOTAL LIABILITIES

A simple subtraction gives you the value of your Estate.

ASSETS — LIABILITIES = NET WORTH

If you are married and hold all property jointly with your spouse, divide by 2 to get the value of your own Net Worth.

Your Net Worth is the value of all that you own, and that is how much your beneficiaries can inherit. Who will inherit your property depends on how your property is *titled* (held or owned).

There are three basic ways to title property:
⇨ in *your name only* – or –
⇨ *jointly* with another – or –
⇨ *in trust for* another.

The way your property is titled determines who will inherit that property:

> Property held in your **name only** will be inherited by the beneficiaries named in your Will.
> If you have no Will, the property will go to your heirs according to the Laws of Descent.
>
> Property you hold **jointly with right of survivorship** will go to the surviving joint owner(s) of that property.
>
> Property held in **Trust** will go to those you name as the beneficiary of the Trust.
>
> **NOTE** ⇨ If you are married, your spouse may have rights in your property, regardless of the way your property is titled.

We will examine each of these types of ownership in detail so that you can give yourself an Estate Planning check-up, i.e., you can check whether the way you are currently holding your property accomplishes your Estate Planning goals.

MINE, ALL MINE

There's much to be said about holding property in your name only and not jointly or in trust for another. There's maximum control. You can sell it, trade it, mortgage it, with no one to account to, or ask "may I?" How you protect your assets depends on how much security you require. Again, it's all up to you.

As discussed, there are three things to consider when setting up an Estate Plan:

CONTROL How to control and protect your Estate during your lifetime.

BENEFICIARY How to be sure your Estate goes to the beneficiary of your choice.

COST How to transfer your Estate to your beneficiaries at lowest cost.

Holding all of your property in your name only should give you maximum control and protection; but such an Estate Plan may present problems with the cost of transferring your property upon your death. More than likely it will take some sort of court procedure to transfer that property once you die. The name of the court procedure is **Probate**. In Virginia, Probate is conducted in the Circuit Court (VA 64.1-75). The Circuit Court also handles other civil and criminal matters. For simplicity, we will refer to the court that handles Probate as the **Probate Court**. We will refer to property that is transferred to your beneficiary by means of a Probate procedure as your **Probate Estate**, and the person appointed by the Court to settle the Estate as your **Personal Representative**.

Probate can be expensive. If you keep all of your property in your name only there could be a significant cost to transfer your property to the beneficiary of your Estate.

Holding property in your name should not create a problem with having your choice of beneficiary inherit your Estate, provided you have a valid Will. But if you die without a Will, the Probate Court will use the Laws of Descent to determine who gets your property. Of course it could be that the beneficiaries of your Estate under the Laws of Descent are exactly who you would have wanted, had you taken the time to prepare a Will. To help you determine if this is the case, we will take a few pages to explain the Law. Those who have a Will might be tempted to skip over the section, but this information is good to know in the event someone in your family dies in Virginia without a Will. Once you read this section you will know whether you have a right to inherit their property.

THE FAMILY'S RIGHT TO INHERIT

The state of Virginia recognizes the right of the family to inherit property left by the **decedent** (the person who died); so the Laws of Intestate Succession cover all possible relationships beginning with the surviving spouse. In order for the spouse to inherit property under the Laws of Intestate Succession, the state of Virginia needs to recognize the union as a valid marriage.

Who Is Your Spouse?

In this era of people challenging the concept of the family unit, those of a philosophical bent may ponder the meaning of marriage. Is it a union of two people in the eyes of God? Is it even a union? Maybe it is just a contract between two people. The Commonwealth of Virginia does not concern itself with such things. If a person dies without a Will, the state will distribute his property according to the laws of Virginia; and the laws of Virginia determine whether two people are married.

BEING MARRIED IN VIRGINIA

To be married in Virginia means that a man and a woman have obtained a license to marry from the state, and then solemnized the marriage by a state or religious ceremony (VA 20-13). Parental consent to marry is required for anyone under 18. If either party is under 16, the Clerk of the Court may not issue a license unless a doctor issues a certificate saying that the woman is pregnant and the parent or Guardian of the person who is under 16 consents to the marriage (VA 20-48).

Virginia law specifically prohibits the marriage of people:
- ☒ whose earlier marriage to another person is still in effect; i.e., bigamy is not allowed;

- ☒ who are *ancestors* (parent, grandparents, etc.) or *descendants* (child, grandchild, etc.) of each other;

- ☒ who are aunt and nephew or uncle and niece regardless of whether related through half or whole blood;

- ☒ who are brother and sister. This includes adopted siblings, regardless of fact that they are not blood relatives (VA 20-38.1).

Virginia law does not bar marriages between cousins.

THE COMMON LAW MARRIAGE

A common law marriage is one that has not been solemnized by ceremony. It is more than just living together. The couple must agree to live together as man and wife, and then publicly hold themselves out as being married; i.e., tell friends and family that they are married. Many states, including Virginia, do not recognize a common law marriage as being valid, and have passed laws to that effect (VA 20-13).

Virginia respects the laws of other states, so even though common law marriages are no longer valid in Virginia, Courts have ruled that they will recognize a common law marriage if it is valid in the state where the couple entered into the marriage (*Kelderhaus v. Kelderhaus*, 21 Va. App.721 (1996)).

NO SAME SEX MARRIAGES

There has been much discussion about whether the state should recognize marriage between people of the same sex. Vermont was the first state to recognize same sex marriages which they refer to as a "civil union." Several states, including Virginia, have passed statutes, specifically denying marital status to couples of the same gender regardless of whether that marriage is valid in any other state (VA 20-45.2).

Now that you know whether the State of Virginia considers you to be married, the next question is whether the state recognizes anyone as your descendant.

Who Is Your Child?

Medical technology has made important contributions to solving the problem of infertility. There are all sorts of solutions, from hormone therapy, to sperm banks that provide donations anonymously, to frozen sperm or ova to be thawed and used at a later date, to women who become a surrogate or gestational mother. Solving a set of medical problems opened the door to a new set of legal problems.

Used to be, the only question was "Who's the father?" Now it could well be "Who's the mother?

To answer these questions, the Commonwealth of Virginia has passed laws (VA 20-156 to 20-165) to legally establish the parentage of children whose conception was assisted by medical technology. We will examine the law as it relates to the right of the child to inherit property.

ASSISTED CONCEPTION

A child born to a married couple using any other form of assisted conception has the same rights as a child conceived the old fashioned way. It is presumed that the husband consented to the assisted conception procedure. If that is not the case, and he is not the father of the child, he can *petition* (ask) the court to terminate his parental rights and responsibilities. He must do this within two years after he discovered (or reasonably should have discovered) that she used assisted conception. If the husband is successful, then the child cannot inherit from his father, and vice versa, the father and his family cannot inherit from the child (VA 20-158).

FROZEN SPERM AND THE AFTERBORN CHILD

Under Virginia law a child conceived prior to death and born to the surviving spouse after the death, has the same right to inherit as any other natural child of the decedent (VA 64.1-8.1). But suppose the child was conceived after death? That question is becoming more of an issue as couples are freezing sperm, ovum or preembryo (fertilized cell) for use at a later date. Often the procedure is done to protect the cell from damage during cancer treatments. If the treatment is unsuccessful, the surviving parent may decide to go ahead with the pregnancy using the frozen reproductive cell. This raises issues of whether the surviving parent has the right to do that without the written consent of the deceased donor; and whether a child born of such procedure is entitled to inherit from the deceased donor.

This inheritance issue has important consequences, not only on the state level but on the federal level as well. A minor child who has lost a parent is entitled to Social Security benefits, but those benefits are based on the state's Laws of Intestate Succession. In Maryland, those laws are called the Laws of Descent and Distribution.

Section 216 of the Social Security Act provides "a child's insurance benefits can be paid to a child who could inherit under the State's intestate laws." Specifically, a child cannot receive Social Security benefits, unless the child is entitled to inherit under the state's Laws of Intestate Succession.

This issue was brought before the Superior Court in New Jersey. The Court ruled that a child conceived and born after the death of a parent can inherit under New Jersey's Laws of Intestate Succession (*In Re Estate of Kolacy*, 322 N.J.Super. 593 (2000)). Other states, including Virginia have passed laws on the issue. Under Virginia law, if a sperm or ovum is preserved, and the donor dies before fertilization takes place, then the deceased donor is not considered as the legal parent of the child unless:

(a)   the procedure took place before there was reasonable notice of the death - or -

(b)   the donor agreed, in writing, to be the parent before the implantation took place.
(VA 20-158, 64.1-8.1).

Those who wish to freeze their reproductive cells, should express in writing, whether the cells can be used after the death of the donor and whether any child born of those reproductive cells shall be considered as a child of the deceased donor and entitled to inherit his Estate.

For those who are married, it is important that your spouse join in the writing and agree to honor your wishes. The written agreement should include a provision about what will be done with the cells in the event of a divorce or the death of either party.

THE SURROGATE PARENTING CONTRACT

Still another legal issue raised because of modern technology is the question of the rights of the Surrogate mother as opposed to the rights of the biological parent who contracted with the Surrogate to bear his/her child.

A Surrogate Parenting Contract is an agreement, usually between a married couple and a woman, in which the woman agrees to be the birth mother of a child conceived with the sperm of the husband, or the egg cell of the wife, or the embryo of the married couple. This means that the husband or wife is the biological parent of the child born of the Surrogate mother.

Some states such as New York and Michigan consider Surrogate Parenting Contracts as being against public policy and have passed laws restricting their use. Virginia has no such prohibition. Virginia statute 20-160 gives the intended parents and the gestational parents, the opportunity to have a Court approve their surrogacy contract. If the parties get Court approval, within 60 days of the child's birth, a new birth certificate is issued by the State Registrar, naming the intended parents as the child's parents.

Things get complicated if the parties do not obtain Court approval of their surrogacy contract, especially if the intended parent or the surrogate has a change of heart. It is beyond the scope of this book to go into all of the "what ifs." The statute is fairly simple to read if you are interested. We'll just take the best case scenario where all of the parties live up to the surrogate agreement. In that case, if one of the intended parents is also a genetic parent, i.e., one of them contributed a sperm or ovum, they can ask the Court to have a new birth certificate issued naming the intended parents as the child's parents.

The parties need to go through an adoption procedure if neither of intended parent is the genetic parent. Once the adoption is complete, the child has the same right to inherit as does any adopted child (VA 20-159, 20-160, 20-162).

THE ADOPTED CHILD

An adopted person who was a minor at the time of adoption has the same right to inherit property under the Laws of Intestate Success from his adoptive parents as does a natural child. The adopted child has no right to inherit from his natural parents, with the exception of the natural parent who is married to the adoptive parent. For example, if a child loses a parent and is later adopted by a step-parent, the child has the right to inherit from his natural parents and from his adoptive parent as well (VA 64.1-5.1).

THE NON-MARITAL CHILD

A child born out of wedlock has the same rights to inherit from his/her natural father as does one born in wedlock, provided:

☑ the decedent participated in a marriage ceremony with the child's mother, before or after the birth, regardless of whether the ceremony resulted in a valid marriage in the state of Virginia - or -

☑ paternity was established by clear and convincing evidence.

If the decedent denied his paternity, then it will take a Court procedure to establish (or disprove) paternity. To inherit property from the decedent, the child, or someone acting on behalf of the child, will need to file an *Affidavit* (a sworn, written statement) with the Clerk stating that the decedent is the child's parent; and at the same time file a petition asking the Court to determine whether the decedent was the child's father (VA 64.1-5.1).

Now that we know who the Commonwealth of Virginia considers to be your spouse, and who is considered your child, we can determine how much of your Probate Estate each is entitled to inherit under Virginia's Laws of Descent and Distribution.

Once your debts, funeral expenses, and the cost of the Probate procedure is paid, whatever is left (your net Probate Estate) is distributed as follows:

✧ MARRIED, NO CHILD OR ALL CHILDREN OF SPOUSE

If at the time of death you are married and have no surviving descendants (child, grandchild, great-grandchild, etc.) — or — if all of your descendents are also descendants of your spouse (i.e., you had them together), then all of your Probate Estate goes to your surviving spouse.

✧ CHILD, NO SPOUSE

If you are single, your children inherit your Probate Estate, in equal shares, *per stirpes*, meaning that if all of your children are alive, they each take an equal share of your net Probate Estate; but if a child dies before you do, then the share intended for the deceased child goes to his/her children, in equal shares. If the deceased child died without leaving a descendant, your surviving children are entitled to an equal share of your Estate (VA 64.1-1, 64.1-3, 64.1-11).

✧ MARRIED, CHILD NOT OF SURVIVING SPOUSE

If you are survived by a descendant who is not a descendant of your spouse (i.e. you had a child with someone who is not your surviving spouse), your spouse gets one-third of your **real property** (land, condominium, home, etc.) The remaining two-thirds goes to your children in equal shares, per stirpes. As for your personal property (money, securities, car etc.), your surviving spouse is entitled to keep up to $10,000 as Exempt Property. The remaining personal property is divided with one-third going to your spouse and the remaining two-thirds to your descendants, per stirpes.

✧ NO CHILD, NO SPOUSE

If you have no spouse and no descendants, then your property will be divided equally between your parents. If only one parent is alive, then all of the property goes to that parent. If neither parent is alive, then your Probate Estate goes to your brothers and sisters in equal shares, per stirpes.

RELATIVES OF HALF-BLOOD INHERIT HALF

Relatives of half-blood inherit half as much as a relative of whole blood. For example, if you are survived by a brother from the same set of parents and a sister with the same father but a different mother, your sister will get half as much as your brother. Your Probate Estate will be divided into three equal shares. Your brother will inherit 2 shares (i.e., two-thirds of your Estate) and your sister will get one share (i.e., one-third of your Estate) (VA 64.1-2).

✧ NO SPOUSE, CHILD, SIBLING OR THEIR DESCENDANT

If you have no spouse, child, sibling, or their descendants, then your Probate Estate is divided with half going to your grandparents (or to the survivor) on your mother's side. If neither maternal grandparent is alive, the property goes to their descendants in equal shares, per stirpes. If they have no surviving descendant, then the half intended for the maternal grandparents (or their descendants) goes to your paternal grandparents (or their descendants).

The paternal half is distributed in the same manner; i.e., half of your Estate goes to your grandparents (or to the survivor) on your father's side. If neither paternal grandparent is alive, then the property goes to their descendants in equal shares, per stirpes. If there are no surviving descendants, then the entire Probate Estate goes to your maternal grandparents (or their descendants) (VA 64.1-1).

NO KINFOLK, BUT RELATIVES OF A DECEASED SPOUSE

If you die leaving absolutely no surviving relative, but your deceased spouse has surviving kinsfolk, your Probate Estate is distributed as if your spouse was entitled to the entire Estate, and died without a Will.

VIRGINIA: HEIR OF LAST RESORT

All unclaimed property goes to the Virginia Department of Treasury, so if you die without a Will and you have absolutely no next of kin, or even if you have a Will and no beneficiary can be found, then the Commonwealth of Virginia "inherits" your Estate (VA 64.1-12).

IT ISN'T ALL THAT SIMPLE

The explanation in this book of the Laws of Intestate Succession is abridged. Even though you may now know more about Virginia's Laws of Descent than you ever wanted to know, there is much more to the law. For example, Virginia statute requires that an heir survive the decedent by at least 120 hours (five days) in order to inherit property under the state's Laws of Descent. If an heir does not live for at least five days after the decedent's death, his property is distributed as if the heir died first. This rule also applies to property inherited by Will, unless the Will makes some different provision. The rule does not apply if it would result in the Commonwealth taking the property (VA 64.1-104.2, 64.1-104.3, 64.1-104.6).

THE COST OF PROBATE

Holding property in your name only gives you maximum control and protection during your lifetime. If you do not like the way your property will be distributed should you die without a Will, then you can control who inherits your property by preparing a Will. But there is still the question of what it will cost to transfer your Estate to your beneficiaries. In all probability, a Probate procedure will be necessary. How much of your Estate will need to be spent to Probate your Estate?

THE SMALL ESTATE

There is no need to be concerned about the cost of Probate if your Estate $15,000 or less. The beneficiary of your Estate can get possession of your property by giving the person who holds the property a SMALL ESTATE AFFIDAVIT. An Affidavit is a written statement in which the *Affiant* (the person making the statement) tells someone with authority to administer an oath (usually a Notary Public) that the statements in the Affidavit are true and correct.

To use the Small Estate Affidavit, the Affiant must verify that the following facts are true:
- ☑ The net value of the decedent's personal property is not greater than $15,000.
- ☑ No Probate procedure is pending.
- ☑ Sixty days have passed since the death.

Your beneficiary can take the Affidavit to whoever has possession of your property (bank, securities broker, etc.) and they will turn over the property to the beneficiary (VA 6.1-71, 64.1-123, 64.1-123.1, 64.1-124.1).

Things are not so simple if you have property in your name only in excess of $15,000. There will need to be a Probate proceeding that can be involved and time consuming; not to mention, expensive. Administration of the Estate can take anywhere from several months to more than a year, depending on the size and complexity of the Estate. The procedure can begin as soon as someone is appointed as Personal Representative. But before someone is appointed the *Virginia Probate Tax* must be paid.

THE PROBATE TAX

A Probate Tax must be paid before anyone can be appointed as Personal Representative. The amount paid is based on the estimated value of the Probate Estate. The final tax is set once the value of the Probate Estate is determined. The Probate Tax is 10 cents for each $100 of property transferred to a beneficiary either through the decedent's Will or through the Virginia Laws of Descent and Distribution. The tax applies to property located within Virginia. It does not apply to real property located in another state or country. And there is no Probate Tax if the decedent's Estate is $10,000 or less.

Incidentally, the Probate Tax, and all other Estate Taxes, must be paid regardless of whether there is a full Probate procedure (VA 58.1-1712, 58.1-1713, 58.1-1715).

Estate Taxes must be taken into account as part of your overall Estate Plan, because taxes are part of the cost of transferring your property to your beneficiary. For most of us, Estate Taxes are not much of a concern because none need be paid unless the Estate is sizeable.

We will discuss Estate Taxes in detail in Chapter 3.

THE PERSONAL REPRESENTATIVE'S FEE

Settling an Estate can be complicated. The Personal Representative must take an inventory of all of the decedent's assets. He may need to employ an appraiser to determine the value of the property. The Personal Representative must identify the decedent's creditors and give them an opportunity to come forward and present their claims. Once the taxes, valid claims and expenses of the administration are paid, the Personal Representative will do an accounting, distribute the assets to the proper beneficiary and then close the Estate.

All of the taxes, claims and expenses are paid from the Probate Estate and not from the Personal Representative's pocket; but if the Personal Representative makes a mistake, he may be made to pay for that mistake. He can be liable if he does not perform his duties as required by law. For example, if he does not file tax returns correctly or on time, he may be responsible to pay for fines levied against the Estate because of his error (VA 26-5). If he distributes your Estate before all taxes are paid, he becomes personally liable for those taxes (VA 58.1-909).

The Personal Representative needs to employ an attorney to guide him through the process. It then becomes the job of the attorney for the Personal Representative to see to it that the Estate is administered properly and without any personal liability to the Personal Representative. The cost of employing an attorney is a proper charge to the Estate.

The Personal Representative is entitled to a reasonable fee for administering the Estate. It is not unusual for the Personal Representative to charge 5% of the value of the Estate for his services. It is not unusual for his attorney to also charge 5%.

THE COST OF A FULL PROBATE PROCEDURE

The Personal Representative and attorney's fees are significant charges to the Probate Estate; but they are not the only charges against the Estate. A Probate procedure can incur some or all of the following expenses:

$$ Court fees to file the Probate procedure

$$ The cost of a bond that the Court may order for the protection of your Probate Estate

$$ The cost of notifying your creditors which may include publishing notice, or mailing notice to them by registered or certified mail

$$ The cost of an appraisal

$$ Accounting fees to prepare an inventory, and account for monies spent during the Probate procedure

$$ The cost of transferring property to the proper beneficiary; i.e., recording fees, broker fees to sell securities or real estate

Once the above costs, Personal Representative fees, attorney fees, taxes and all valid claims, are paid, the Personal Representative will distribute whatever is left to the proper beneficiary and then close the Estate.

You may be thinking that Probate is a good thing to avoid. Why should your Personal Representative go through all that effort to settle your Estate? Why should your beneficiaries wait months or maybe years, and pay all these fees to inherit your Estate?

There are ways to arrange your Estate so that your beneficiaries can immediately inherit your Estate without incurring unnecessary costs. In the next two chapters we will examine different methods that can be used to achieve this goal.

Is Probate Necessary? 2

Many people think that only wealthy people need to make plans to avoid Probate, yet each year, heirs of relatively modest estates, spend thousands of dollars to settle an Estate. A bit of Estate Planning could have eliminated most, if not all, of the cost (and hassle) suffered by those families.

If you have a small Estate and only one or two beneficiaries, then it is not all that difficult to arrange your finances to eliminate the need for Probate altogether. All you need do is title your property so that it automatically goes to your beneficiaries. There are many ways to arrange your finances to get this result. The most common method is to hold property jointly with another. Such an arrangement is the Estate Plan of choice for most married couples. Husband and wife often hold all of their property jointly, so that the surviving spouse has complete and immediate access to their property without any need for Probate.

Holding property jointly may not be the most desirable method for the single person, or for the surviving spouse who is now single. There are other ways to ensure that your property is inherited quickly and without cost to your heirs. In this chapter we explore the pros and cons of different methods of holding property so that it can be transferred without the need for Probate.

PROPERTY OWNED JOINTLY

Bank accounts, securities, motor vehicles, real property can all be owned by two or more people. If one of the owners dies, the survivor(s) continue to own their share of the property. Who owns the share belonging to the decedent depends on Virginia law and how ownership of the property was set up.

THE JOINT BANK ACCOUNT

When a bank account is opened in two or more names, the owners of the account sign an agreement with the bank stating who is to have access to the account during the lifetime of the account owners; i.e. whether each owner has full authority to make a withdrawal, or whether two signatures are required. The agreement should also state how the ownership of the account is to be transferred should one of the owners die. If the agreement says that there are **Rights of Survivorship**, then upon the death of one account owner, the remaining joint owner(s) will own the account. Unless the agreement with the bank states differently, it is presumed that each joint owner is an equal owner of the account and the decedent's share is to be divided equally between them.

If there is no Right of Survivorship, the share of the account that belongs to the decedent goes to whomever he named in his Will. If he left no Will, his share will go to his next of kin as determined by the Virginia Laws of Descent.

TITLE TO A JOINT ACCOUNT IN VIRGINIA

Joint accounts opened in Virginia after July 1, 2000 must clearly state JOINT ACCOUNTS WITH SURVIVORSHIP or JOINT ACCOUNT — NO SURVIVORSHIP. Accounts opened prior to that date, or out of state accounts, might not be so specific. The word "Joint" or "Jointly," without any indication of survivorship, does not necessarily mean that the money belongs to the surviving owners. If you have any question about whether your joint account has Rights of Survivorship, ask the bank to show you the contract that you signed when you opened the account (VA 6.1-125.1, 6.1-125.15).

Once an owner of a joint account dies, the surviving owner is free to withdraw all of the monies from the account without the need to go through any Probate procedure to get that money; but understanding that he may be responsible to pay Probate Taxes if the amount he inherits from the account is greater than $10,000 (see page 20); and also understanding that if there is a Probate proceeding, the Personal Representative has the right to ask the surviving joint owner to contribute as much from the decedent's share of the account as is necessary to settle the decedent's Estate (see Chapter 5).

Most married couples hold their bank accounts as a joint account with survivorship, so that should one become incapacitated or die, the other will have immediate access to the account. Some parents set up a joint account with survivorship with their child, to avoid the need for Probate of that account, but that may not be the best Estate Plan.

⊠ OVERREACHING

Making your child a joint owner of the account gives the child free access to the account. Monies may be withdrawn without your knowledge or authorization. You may be thinking that couldn't happen because you would immediately know of the withdrawal, and you could force the child to return the money. That may be true when you are healthy and alert. But in this ever aging society, it is likely that you will live to an advanced age and not be as aware as you are today. And if you have two children and decided to hold your account jointly with them, then there may be a problem with how the funds are distributed should you die.

That was the case with Amanda. All she had when her husband died, was a bank account worth $50,000. She wanted to be sure that the money would go to her two sons, Robert and Leon, without the need for Probate. She went to the bank with her two sons and opened a new survivorship account with all three names on the account as joint owners.

Several years passed without incident. As Amanda aged, her health began to fail, and she became more and more dependent on Robert. She needed his assistance to take her to the doctor, to do her shopping, and of course take care of her finances. Robert had a wife and two children, so it was hard for him to care for his family and his mother as well.

Leon was single, yet he never seemed to have the time to help care for his mother. And Robert resented that.

Finally, Amanda died.

After the funeral, Leon asked Robert about the bank account "Didn't Mom have a joint account in our names?"

"Yeah, but I closed it out. There was only a few thousand left, and I used it for her funeral."

Leon thought it strange that all of the money was gone, so he went to the bank and asked to see the record of withdrawals. He found that over the last two years Robert had written several large checks to himself. There was only $7,000 left in the account when Robert closed it out, within a week of her death.

Leon fumed for several weeks before he brought up the subject. Robert's face flushed when Leon asked about the money. Leon did not know if it was from anger or embarrassment. He soon learned that it was both when Robert asked "Where were you for the past two years? You never once helped. Did you know she became incontinent at the end? Who cleaned up? Not you. She blessed me every day. She often said she would have been dead long ago if it wasn't for me. She wanted me to have that money!"

"Mom never said anything to me about wanting you to have the money. She never asked for my help and neither did you. It isn't right for you to throw this up to me now."

The boys never spoke of the money again. But then there were few times that they ever spoke to each other after that.

Overreaching isn't the only problem with a joint account, there is also the problem of liability.

⊠   POTENTIAL LIABILITY

If you hold a bank account jointly with your adult child and that child is sued or gets a divorce, the child may need to disclose his ownership of the joint account. In such a case, you may find yourself spending money to prove that the account was established for convenience only and that all of the money in that account really belongs to you.

Because of these inherent problems, you might want to hold the funds so that your beneficiary does not have access to the monies unless you die while the account is open. You can do so by opening a *Beneficiary Account*.

THE BENEFICIARY ACCOUNT

As explained, the terms of a bank account are established when a bank account is opened. Your agreement gives directions about who can access your account during your lifetime, but it can also give directions about what to do with the account should you die. If you hold the account in your name only and do not give any such directions, then should you die while the account is open, the monies in your account will become part of your Probate Estate and will be distributed in the same way as any other item that you hold in your name only.

One way to avoid Probate of the account, yet retain full control of the account during your lifetime, is to name one or more persons to be the beneficiary of your account.

There are two forms of beneficiary account. Your contract with the bank can direct the bank to hold your account *In Trust For* ("ITF") one or more beneficiaries that you name; or you can have a contract with the bank that directs the bank to *Pay On Death* ("POD") all of the money in the account to one or more beneficiaries that you name

If you open an ITF or POD account , then under Virginia law, unless your agreement with the bank says differently:

⇨   During your lifetime you are free to change beneficiaries without asking the beneficiary's permission to do so.

⇨   The beneficiary does not have access to the account during your lifetime (VA 6.1-125.1).

You can open a Pay On Death account with instructions to give the money to your child when you die, and if the child dies before you, then to your grandchildren in equal shares. For example:

Eldon Connors POD Betty Connors LDPS

which is short-hand for:

"ELDON CONNORS is the owner of the account. Upon his death, pay the money in the account to BETTY CONNORS, but if she dies first, then give it to her lineal descendants, in equal shares, per stirpes" (VA 64.1-206.8).

There may be times when you wish to hold an account jointly (say with your spouse) and have your children inherit the money when you both die. For example:

ELDON CONNORS and LORRAINE CONNORS,
JOINT ACCOUNT WITH SURVIVORSHIP, POD
JAMES CONNORS, JR. AND FRED CONNORS

Under Virginia law, unless the agreement with the bank says differently:

⇨ The children (James. and Fred) have no right to the account during the lifetime of their parents.

⇨ If either parent dies, the surviving parent owns the account, and is free to close the account or change the beneficiary of the account.

⇨ Once both parents are deceased, their sons will own an equal share in the account.

⇨ If one of the children dies before his parent, the remaining son gets all of the money in the account (VA 6.1-125.5).

THE TRANSFER ON DEATH SECURITY

The Virginia law for securities is similar to the statute for bank accounts in that you can arrange to have a security (a stock, bond or securities account) transferred to a beneficiary upon your death. You can instruct the holder of the security to **Transfer On Death** ("TOD") to a named beneficiary. As with the POD designation, the TOD registration has no effect on the ownership of the security until the owner of the security dies. For example:

TANYA BEDDIE TOD LUCINDA BEDDIE

Once Tanya dies, all Lucinda need do is produce a certified copy of the death certificate and the security will be transferred to Lucinda. Should Lucinda die before Tanya, then the security will become part of Tanya's estate (VA 64.1-206.4).

If a security is owned jointly and the owners wish to have someone inherit the property when they both die, Virginia law requires that they hold the security as Joint Tenants with Rights of Survivorship; i.e., the beneficiary cannot inherit the security until they both die. This is a convenient way of owning a security for the married couple who want a child to inherit the security without going through a Probate procedure. For example, the security can be titled as:

TIM REILLY and OLIVIA REILLY, JOINT TENANTS
WITH SURVIVORSHIP TOD STUART REILLY

Should both parents die, Stuart will inherit the security. If Stuart dies before his parents, then the security will go to the estate of the last parent to die (VA 64.1-206.2, 64.1-206.5).

If your Estate consists only of bank accounts and/or securities, and you want all of your property to go to one or two beneficiaries without the need for Probate, but with maximum control and protection of your funds during your lifetime, then holding your property in any of these beneficiary forms:

In Trust For

Pay On Death

Transfer On Death

should accomplish your goal.

REAL PROPERTY OWNED JOINTLY

If you own real property together with another, then who will own the property upon your death depends on how the current owner is identified on the face of the deed. The first paragraph of the deed should identify the person who transferred the property to you (the **Grantor**). The person to whom the property was transferred is called the **Grantee** (VA 55-48). The deed might read something like:

This deed made the 14th day of August, 2004
between ROBERT TRAYNOR, a single man
hereinafter referred to as the GRANTOR
and
SUSAN CODY, a married woman
and HENRY TRAYNOR, a single man,
as **Co-owners with Right of Survivorship**
hereinafter referred to as the GRANTEE
. . .

Robert Traynor is the Grantor of the deed. That means he transferred the property to Susan Cody and Henry Traynor who are the Grantees and the present owners of the property. Robert transferred the property to Susan and Henry as CO-OWNERS WITH RIGHT OF SURVIVORSHIP. Should one of them die, the other will own the property 100%. The survivor need do nothing to establish the ownership, but both names remain on the deed. Later in the chapter we will explain what documents should be recorded to let everyone know that there is just one remaining owner (VA 64.1-104.1).

▤ DEED HELD AS TENANTS IN COMMON

You might have a deed that names you and another person as Grantee, followed by **TENANTS IN COMMON**. In such case, there are no Rights of Survivorship. Should you die, your share of the property will go to whomever you named as beneficiary of that share in your Will. If you die without a Will, the Virginia Laws of Descent and Distribution determine who inherits the property.

Under Virginia law, there is no Right of Survivorship unless the deed says so; i.e., a deed that identifies the Grantees as **JOINT TENANTS**, but does not say that there is a **RIGHT OF SURVIVORSHIP**, is a Tenancy In Common (VA 55-20).

▤ DEED HELD AS HUSBAND AND WIFE

A married couple who hold property as follows:
   TODD AMES AND SUSAN AMES, TENANTS BY THE ENTIRETY
have Rights of Survivorship. When one spouse dies, and providing they are married at the time of death, the surviving spouse owns the property 100%. As with property owned jointly with Right of Survivorship, nothing need be done to establish that ownership, but it is a good idea to have documents recorded showing that the surviving spouse is now the sole owner.

If a husband and wife own real property and the deed does not say **TENANTS BY THE ENTIRETY**, or does not say that they have a **RIGHT OF SURVIVORSHIP**, then they hold title as **TENANTS IN COMMON** (VA 55-20.1).

DEED WITH A LIFE ESTATE

A *Life Estate* interest in real property means that the person who owns the Life Estate has the right to live in that property until he/she dies. You can identify a Life Estate interest by examining the face of the deed. If somewhere on the face of the deed you see the phrase RESERVING A LIFE ESTATE, the Grantee cannot take possession of the property until the owner of the Life Estate dies. For example, suppose the granting paragraph of the deed reads:

This deed made this day, January 15, 2005, between ROSE CAVALLO, a single woman, Grantor and SALVATORE CAVALLO, a married man, Grantee

Witnesseth: that said Grantor doth grant unto the said Grantee all of the property described as ......

RESERVING A LIFE ESTATE TO THE GRANTOR

. . .

Rose is the owner of the Life Estate. Salvatore is the owner of the *Remainder Interest*. Rose has the right to occupy the premises during her lifetime or to rent it out and receive the income from the property. During Rose's lifetime, Salvatore has no right to the possession of, or the income from, the property. Once Rose dies, Salvatore will own the property and is free to take possession of the property and to lease, sell or transfer it, as he sees fit.

If you are an owner of the Life Estate interest, upon your death, no Probate procedure will be necessary to transfer the property to the owner of the Remainder Interest.

TRANSFERRING REAL PROPERTY

In Virginia, and most other states, no Probate procedure is necessary to transfer real property if the decedent held the property:

⇨ as the owner of a Life Estate — or —

⇨ Co-owner with Right of Survivorship — or —

⇨ as Tenants By The Entirety (i.e., as husband and wife)

The surviving party owns the property as of the decedent's date of death, but the decedent's name remains on the deed. In Virginia, the State Registrar of Vital Statistics keeps a record of the death, but the Registrar does not publish the death certificate so it is not part of the public record (VA 32.1-252). Anyone who examines title to the property will not know of the death unless a document is recorded in the county where the property is located. This is not a problem if the beneficiary of the property intends to sell or transfer the property. All the beneficiary need do is produce a certified copy of the death certificate at closing.

If the beneficiary does not intend to sell or transfer the property in the near future, he can have documentation recorded showing that he is the surviving owner. That is done by going to the Clerk of the Circuit Court in the city or county where the property is located. The Clerk will give the beneficiary an Affidavit to sign giving notice of the death. Once signed, the Clerk will record the document and send an abstract of the Affidavit to the Commissioner of Revenue, who will then indicate the new ownership of the property on the Land Books. Once the change is recorded, anyone who examines the title to the property will know of the change of ownership (VA 64.1-135).

Much the same procedure is followed for property held in the decedent's name only, or as a Tenant in Common. If the decedent died without a Will, then the decedent's Personal Representative needs to complete an Affidavit provided by the Clerk of the Circuit Court. The Affidavit will state the legal description of the property, and the names and last known addresses of the decedent's heirs. The Clerk will record the Affidavit and send an abstract of the Affidavit to the Commissioner of Revenue. If it is not necessary to conduct a Probate proceeding, the person who inherits the property can sign the Clerk's Affidavit, and have the property transferred after paying the Probate Tax.

No Affidavit is necessary if the decedent left a valid Will. Once the Will is admitted to Probate, the Clerk will give the Personal Representative a certified copy of the Will. The Personal Representative needs to have the certified copy of the Will recorded in each county where the decedent's real property is located (VA 55-6, 64.1-94).

If the decedent's Will was probated in another state, then a copy that is certified in the other state is not sufficient. The Clerk will require that the out of state Will be admitted to Probate in the county where the property is located. Once the Will is admitted to Probate in Virginia, the Clerk of the Probate Court will issue a certified copy of the Will that can be recorded in any Virginia county where real property owned by the decedent is located (VA 64.1-92).

If you own real property in your name only, then once you die, your beneficiary might be able to transfer the property without any need for Probate. Virginia is unique in that you may be able to transfer real property without going through a full Probate procedure, but if you have more than $15,000 in personal property, then Probate is necessary. Many other states are just the opposite. They have a relatively simple procedure for transferring personal property, but require a full Probate procedure for the transfer of real property.

OUT OF STATE PROPERTY

This chapter relates only to property that you own in Virginia. If you own property in another state or country, then the laws of that state or country determine who has the right to inherit property in that state. Whether or not there are Rights of Survivorship depend on the laws of the state. Some states, like Virginia, require that the deed specify whether there are Rights of Survivorship. In other states, a deed held Joint Tenancy has Rights of Survivorship even if the deed does not specify such right. If you own out of state property jointly with another, it is important that you check with an attorney in that state to be sure that your share of the property will go to the person of your choice.

In many states a surviving spouse has rights in real property owned by a decedent spouse, even though the deed was in the decedent's name only. If you are married and hold property in another state your spouse may have rights in that property even though only your name appears on the deed.

Still another concern is whether a Probate procedure will be necessary to transfer that property to your beneficiary. If you own property in your name only in this state and in another state, upon your death it may be necessary to have a Probate proceeding in Virginia, and an *ancillary* (secondary) Probate proceeding in the state where the property is located. This can double the cost of Probate.

And there is the matter of taxes. Some states have an inheritance tax in addition to an Estate Tax. Taxes may be due in the state where the property is located as well as in Virginia. It may be necessary to file a tax return in two states. In addition to increased taxes, this can significantly increase the cost of accounting fees.

If you own property in another state, it is important to consult with an attorney to learn the answers to all of these questions, namely:

> *Who will inherit my property under the laws of the state where it is located?*

> *Will a Probate procedure be necessary to transfer that property to my beneficiaries?*

> *What taxes will need to be paid in that state?*

THE COST OF AVOIDING PROBATE

If you find that Probate will be necessary to transfer real property that you own in Virginia or elsewhere, you may decide that the cost of Probate is too expensive. You may be tempted to go for the quick fix of having the deed to the property changed so that you are joint owners with the intended beneficiary of the property; or you may decide to transfer the property to your intended beneficiary and keep a Life Estate for yourself.

This will avoid Probate, but it may not be the best Estate Plan because you will not have maximum control over the property during your lifetime. If you hold real property as a Joint Tenant or as a Life Tenant, you will not be able to sell that property during your lifetime without getting permission from your beneficiary. And if the beneficiary gives permission and the property is sold, the beneficiary will have the legal right to share in the proceeds of the sale.

You may be thinking "I can make my son joint owner of my home and avoid any need for Probate. I trust him to do what I want with the property. If I decide to sell, I know he won't ask for any part of the proceeds regardless of his legal right to those funds."

And all that may be true, but it may cost you more in taxes to sell your property than if you kept the property in your name only.

Under today's law, you can sell your home without paying a Capital Gains Tax, provided you lived there for 2 of the prior 5 years and the Capital Gains on the sale is not greater than $250,000 ($500,000 if married). If you sell your home after making the Life Estate transfer (or making your child a Joint Tenant), then unless your child occupies the home as his primary residence, his share of the property is subject to a Capital Gains Tax.

If your son does not take his share of the proceeds, then why should he pay any Capital Gains Tax?

In such case, you'll be the one to pay the tax on your son's share of the proceeds.

Is there a better way to avoid Probate?

Maybe. Read on.

How To Avoid Probate   3

TRUE OR FALSE?

(   )   If you have a Will, then Probate will be necessary.

(   )   Probate will be necessary if you don't have a Will.

(   )   Probate is necessary if you own property that is worth more than $15,000.

If you answered false to all of the above, you are either a lawyer, or you carefully read the last chapter.

All of these sentences are false because all of your property may pass to your beneficiaries automatically, without the need for Probate, such as property held jointly or in a Pay On Death account. The point we were trying to make is:

> Whether Probate is necessary has nothing to do with whether there is a Will, or even how much money is involved. The determining factor is how the property is titled (owned).

There are three basic ways to title property:

- ✧   in your name only
- ✧   jointly with another
- ✧   in trust for another

Chapter 1 examined the pros and cons of holding property in your name only, with the biggest "con" being that Probate may be necessary.

In Chapter 2 we noted that holding property jointly with another solved the Probate problem, but at the sacrifice of the control and protection offered by keeping property in your name only. In this Chapter we examine another option which may be the solution to these problems, namely the REVOCABLE LIVING TRUST (also known as an *Inter Vivos Trust*).

A Revocable Living Trust is designed to care for your property during your lifetime and then to distribute your property once you die without the need for Probate. You may have been encouraged to set up such a Trust by your financial planner, attorney, or accountant. Even people of modest means are being encouraged to use a Trust as the basis of their Estate Plan. But Trusts also have their pros and cons. Before getting into that, let's first discuss what a Trust is and how it works.

HOW A TRUST IS CREATED

To create a **Revocable Living Trust**, an attorney prepares a Trust Agreement in accordance with the client's needs and desires. The "Agreement" refers to the fact that the person setting up the Trust (the *Trustor* or *Settlor*) is contracting with someone to be the **Trustee** (manager) of property placed in the Trust. By signing the Trust Agreement, the Trustee agrees to manage the Trust property according to the directions given in the Trust Agreement. If the Trustor is the one who places property into the Trust, then he is referred to as the **Grantor.** The Trust Agreement also names a **Successor Trustee** who will take over the management of the Trust property should the Trustee resign, become incapacitated or die.

We will refer to the Revocable Living Trust as the "Living Trust" or just the "Trust" and the person setting up the Trust as the "Grantor." Usually the Grantor appoints himself as the initial Trustee so that he is in total control of property that he places into the Trust. In such case he signs the Trust Agreement as the Grantor and also as the Trustee who agrees to follow the terms of the Trust Agreement.

Once the Trust document is properly signed, the Grantor can transfer property into the Trust. The Grantor does this by changing the name on the account from his individual name to his name as Trustee. For example, if Elaine Richards sets up a Trust naming herself as Trustee, and she wants to put her bank account into the Trust, all she need do is instruct the bank to change the name on the account from Elaine Richards to:

ELAINE RICHARDS, TRUSTEE OF THE ELAINE RICHARDS
REVOCABLE LIVING TRUST
UNDER AGREEMENT DATED JULY 12, 2004.

If Elaine wants to put real property that she owns into the Trust, she can have her attorney or a title insurance company prepare and record a new deed with the owner of the property identified as:

ELAINE RICHARDS, TRUSTEE OF THE ELAINE RICHARDS REVOCABLE TRUST AGREEMENT DATED JULY 12, 2004.

The Trust Agreement states how property placed into the Trust is to be managed during Elaine's lifetime. Elaine, as Trustee, controls the Trust property. For example, monies she keeps in a Trust bank account can be withdrawn or added to in the same manner as if the account were in her name only.

Because the Trust is revocable, Elaine can cancel the Trust at any time and have the Trust property put back into her own name. If Elaine does not revoke the Trust during her lifetime, once she dies the Trust becomes irrevocable. Her Successor Trustee is required to follow the terms of the Trust Agreement as it is written. If the Trust says to give the Trust property to certain beneficiaries, the Successor Trustee will do so; and in most cases without any Probate procedure. If the Trust directs the Successor Trustee to continue to hold property in Trust and use the money to take care of a member of Elaine's family, then it is the job of the Successor Trustee to use the money to care for the family member as directed in the Trust Agreement.

THE PROS AND CONS OF A TRUST

THE GOOD PART
Setting up a Trust has many good features.

☆ AVOID PROBATE
As discussed in Chapter 1, Probate can be time consuming and expensive. Both the Personal Representative and his attorney are entitled to payment for their services. These fees can be significant. It may be necessary to hire accountants and appraisers, as well. If you have property in two states, then two Probate procedures may be necessary (one in each state) and that could have the effect of doubling the cost of Probate. If the Trust is properly drafted and your property placed into the Trust, you should be able to avoid Probate altogether.

☆ AVOID A CHALLENGE TO YOUR ESTATE PLAN
A Trust operates much like a Will because it provides for the distribution of your Estate when you die. Unlike a Will, it is not subject to Probate, so no Court is charged with the duty of "proving" that your Trust is valid. Your Successor Trustee can distribute your property as you direct, without asking anyone's permission to do so, and without giving the Court or any outside party an opportunity to examine the document. This does not mean that your Estate Plan cannot be challenged; but if the Trust is drafted according to Virginia law, and not with the intent of ripping off your creditors, or cutting off your spouse's right to inherit, it will be very difficult for anyone to challenge the document.

☆ PRIVACY

Your Trust is a private document. No one but your Successor Trustee and your beneficiaries need ever read it. When opening a bank account in the name of the Trust, the bank might ask for a copy of the Trust Agreement, but all they need is basic information about the Trust such as the date of execution of the Trust; the Trust tax identification number; the identity of the Grantor, the current Trustee, the identity of Successor Trustee and the beneficiaries of the Trust, etc. You attorney can prepare a *Certificate of Trust* to give to the bank that contains this basic information.

If you have a Will, once it is admitted to Probate it becomes part of the Court record. Your Personal Repre- sentative is required to have a certified copy of your Will recorded in any county where you own real property (VA 64.1-94). Once recorded, the Will becomes a public document. Anyone can examine the county records, read your Will and see who you did (or did not) provide for in your Will. Other Probate documents such as the inventory of your Probate Estate, creditor's claims, etc. are also open to public scrutiny. In many states, Court records are now available on the Internet!

LEASE SAFE DEPOSIT BOX AS TRUSTEE

Another privacy issue is what happens to the contents your safe deposit box, should you become disabled or die. Under Virginia law, if you hold a safe deposit box in your name only, once the bank (or other safe deposit box lessor) learns of your death, access to the box is restricted. Under Virginia law, the bank may allow a spouse or next of kin to look at the contents of the box under the supervision of an officer or employee of the company. If the Will is there, the bank can arrange to have it delivered to the Clerk of the Circuit Court.

Other than the Will, nothing else can be removed from the safe deposit box without authorization from the Clerk of the Circuit Court (VA 6.1-332.1).

By leasing the safe deposit box in your capacity as Trustee, you can avoid having the bank officer (or anyone other than your Successor Trustee) examine the contents of your safe deposit box. You can instruct the bank that upon your death or disability, your Successor Trustee has full authority to enter the box and remove any and all of the items from that box.

☆ CARE FOR FAMILY MEMBER

You can make provision in your Trust to care for a minor child or family member after you die. If your family member is immature or a born spender, and you are concerned that he may spend, within months, what it took you a lifetime to earn, you can have your attorney prepare a Trust that will spread the inheritance over an extended period of time. Your Trust can direct the Trustee to give a certain amount of money every 5 or 10 years; for example you can direct the Trustee to give part of the gift when the beneficiary reaches 25, another amount when he reaches 35, and then 45, etc.

If your intended beneficiary has a creditor problem, you can set up a *Spendthrift Trust*. You can direct your Successor Trustee to use the Trust funds for your beneficiary's health care, education, and living expenses, and nothing else. The Trust funds can be protected from the beneficiary's creditors, but only to a maximum of one million dollars. In Virginia, Trust funds in excess of one million dollars are available to pay for the beneficiary's debts (VA 55-19).

NO CREDITOR PROTECTION FOR GRANTOR

You can set up a Spendthrift Trust for a beneficiary so that the beneficiary's creditors cannot force payment for debts run up by that beneficiary. But you cannot set up a Spendthrift Trust for yourself. Because property held in your Revocable Living Trust is freely accessible to you, it is likewise accessible to your creditors both before and after your death. If you die owing money, your creditors can have a Personal Representative appointed to locate funds to pay those debts. The Personal Representative can require that your Trust property be used to pay for those debts (VA 55-19).

☆☆ AVOID CONSERVATORSHIP

Once you have a Trust you do not need to worry about who will take care of your property should you become disabled or too aged to handle your finances. The person you appoint as Successor Trustee will take over the care of the Trust property if you are unable to do so. If you do not have a Trust and you become incapacitated, a Court may need to appoint a Conservator to care for your property. The cost to establish and maintain the Conservatorship is charged to you. And, as we will see in Chapter 9 that can be even more expensive than a Probate procedure.

With all these perks, you may be ready to call your attorney to make an appointment to set up a Trust, but before doing so there are a few things you need to consider.

THE CONS

☒ COMPLEXITY

A Trust is a fairly complex document, often more than 20 pages long. It needs to be that long because you are establishing a vehicle for taking care of your property during your lifetime, as well as after your death. Your Trust may be written in "legalese," so it may take you considerable time and effort to understand it. It is important to have your Trust document prepared by an attorney who has the patience to work with you until you fully understand each paragraph of the document and are satisfied that what it states is what you really want.

☒ COST

Because of the thoroughness of the document and the fact that it is custom designed for you, a Trust will cost much more to draft than a simple Will. In addition to the initial cost of the Trust, it can be expensive to maintain the Trust should you become disabled or die. Your Successor Trustee has the right to charge for his duties as Trustee, as well as to charge for any specialized services performed. A financial institution can charge to serve as Successor Trustee, and also charge to manage the Trust portfolio. If you decide to have a financial institution serve as Trustee, then it is important that you compare the fee schedules of different institutions.

You can choose an attorney, or an accountant, or a financial planner, to serve as Trustee, but this may create a conflict of interest because the professional can use his position as Trustee to generate fees for himself or his firm. If you decide to appoint a professional as Trustee you should have a fee agreement stating what will be charged for his duties as Trustee and what will be charged for professional work done on behalf of the Trust.

The fee agreement should be included in the Trust document with a provision that whoever accepts the job of Successor Trustee, agrees to accept the fee as provided in the Trust document.

You may decide to appoint your spouse or a family member as Successor Trustee, who may want little, or no, compensation. Regardless of who you choose to be Successor Trustee, you need to come to a fee agreement. The agreement can be for a set amount or a percentage of the value of the Trust, or whatever other method you want to be used to determine his compensation.

If you do not make written provision for fees, then under Virginia law, the Trustee (and his attorney) are entitled to be compensated in the same manner as any other *fiduciary* who operates for the benefit of another, such as a Personal Representative or a Conservator (VA 26-30).

⊠ YOU MAY NEED YOUR SPOUSE'S PERMISSION TO TRANSFER PROPERTY INTO YOUR TRUST

Most married couples prepare a Trust as part of their overall Estate Plan. Sometimes a married person has a Trust that was prepared prior to the marriage, or he may decide to create a Trust to care for children from a previous marriage. In such case, it may be necessary to have the spouse agree, in writing, to transfers into the Trust. The reason permission is needed is the *Elective Share*. The Grantor's spouse has a right to inherit at least as much as allowed under Virginia law, unless the spouse signed a prenuptial or postnuptial agreement giving up that right.

In Virginia, the Elective Share is one-third of the *Augmented Estate* of the decedent spouse. The Augmented Estate includes:

⇨ The Probate Estate after payment of all the costs and expenses of the Probate procedure

⇨ Non-probate transfers (Trust property, joint accounts, In Trust For accounts, Transfer On Death securities, etc.)

⇨ Gifts in excess of $10,000, per person, per year made by the decedent within 5 years of his death (VA 64.1-16.1).

If you make transfers into your Trust without your spouse's permission, and without providing for the Elective Share, your surviving spouse can go to Court and demand that as much property be transferred from the Trust (or from anyone in possession of your property) as is necessary to make up the Elective Share (VA 64.1-16.2).

⊠ PROBATE MIGHT STILL BE NECESSARY

The Trust only works for those items that you place in the Trust. If you own property in your name only, then upon your death, a Probate procedure might be necessary in order to transfer the property to your beneficiary. For example, if you purchase a security in your name only, without a "Transfer On Death" designation to a beneficiary or to your Trust, a Probate procedure may be necessary to determine who should inherit the security.

The attorney who prepares the Trust usually creates a safety net for such situations. He prepares a Will for you to sign at the same time you sign the Trust. The Will makes your Trust the beneficiary of your Probate Estate. If you own anything in your name only, should a Probate procedure be necessary, the Will directs your Personal Representative to make that asset part of your Trust by transferring the asset to your Successor Trustee. Your Successor Trustee will add that asset to your Trust.

The Will prepared by the attorney is called a ***Pour Over Will*** because it is designed to "pour" any asset titled in your name only, into the Trust. Having the Will ensures that all of your property will go to the beneficiaries named in your Trust. But the downside of holding property in your name only is that a full Probate procedure may be necessary just to get that asset into your Trust. If avoiding Probate is your goal, holding property, in your name only, defeats that goal.

You can ensure that a Probate procedure will not be necessary by transferring your assets into your Trust during your lifetime, but if you neglect to put something into your Trust, the Pour Over Will stands by to transfer that asset into your Trust.

☆ ⊠ THE TRUST IS LEGALLY ENFORCEABLE

Any beneficiary of the Trust can petition a Circuit Court to settle a dispute arising out of the administration of the Trust. The Trustee also has the right to petition the Court for authority to do certain things not authorized in the Trust document. For example, the Trustee can ask the Court to issue an order giving the Trustee authority to terminate the Trust and distribute the Trust property to the beneficiaries (VA 26-1, 55-19.4).

We gave this section a cross and a star, because the right to have a Trust enforced or administered by a court is a double edged sword. It is great to have a court protect the rights of your beneficiaries, but the cost of a court battle could be greater than using Probate to transfer your Estate. Worse yet, your beneficiaries are at a disadvantage because the Trustee can charge the legal expenses to your Trust, while the beneficiaries must pay for the battle out of their own pocket.

Even if the beneficiaries win the argument, the Trustee's legal fees are paid from the Trust, so there is just that much less for the beneficiaries to inherit.

Putting property into a Revocable Living Trust does not shield that property from taxes. All of the property held in a Revocable Living Trust is taxed as if the Grantor were holding that property in his/her own name. If the property earns income, then income taxes will be due, and at the same rate as the Grantor would have paid if he had no Trust. Once the Grantor dies, both the federal and state government have the right to impose an *Estate Tax* on property transferred to a beneficiary as a result of the death. All the property owned as of the date of death becomes the decedent's *Taxable Estate.* This includes *real property* (residential lots, condominiums, etc.) and *personal property* (cars, life insurance policies, business interests, securities, IRA accounts, etc.). It includes property held in the decedent's name alone, as well as property that he held jointly or in Trust. It also includes gifts given by the decedent during his lifetime that exceeded $10,000 per person, per year. In the year 2002, the *Annual Gift Tax Exclusion* of $10,000 was increased to $11,000 to adjust for inflation (IRC 2503(b)).

For most of us, this is not a concern because no federal or Virginia Estate Tax need be paid unless the decedent's Taxable Estate exceeds the federal *Estate Tax Exclusion* amount. That value is currently one and a half million dollars and is scheduled to go even higher.

YEAR	ESTATE TAX EXCLUSION AMOUNT
2004-2005	$1,500,000
2006-2008	$2,000,000
2009	$3,500,000

In 2010 the federal Estate Tax is scheduled to be phased out altogether; however in 2011, the Estate Tax will be reinstated with an Exclusion Amount of $1,000,000 unless lawmakers change the tax law once again.

THE VIRGINIA "PICK-UP" TAX

The Virginia Estate Tax is based on the federal Estate Tax. The federal government imposes a tax on all property transferred because of the death. The federal government then grants an Estate Tax credit, so that no tax need be paid unless the amount transferred is greater than the federal Estate Tax Exclusion amount (currently 1.5 million dollars). The Virginia Estate Tax is called a "pick-up" tax because the state collects taxes that would have gone to the federal government had it not been for the federal Estate Tax credit.

As with the federal Estate Tax, no Estate tax is due to the Commonwealth, unless the decedent's Taxable Estate exceeds the current federal Tax Exclusion amount. But for those Estates that are larger than the Exclusion value, Estate taxes will need to be paid to the federal government and to the state of Virginia. And that includes property transferred within the state regardless of whether the decedent was a resident of Virginia (VA 58.1-902).

The federal Estate Tax is scheduled to be phased out and then reinstated in 2011. The Virginia Estate Tax is based on the federal Estate Tax credit, so unless the state legislature changes things, the Virginia Estate Tax will go the way of the federal Estate Tax.

Both state and federal government do not tax property passing to the decedent's spouse, however, once the surviving spouse dies, all of his/her Estate is subject to Estate taxes. As explained on the next page, setting up a Revocable Living Trust can significantly reduce the amount of federal and Virginia Estate Taxes that may need to be paid once the surviving spouse dies.

A TRUST TO REDUCE ESTATE TAXES

Under current law, Estates of those who die in 2010 are exempt from Federal Estate taxes, but in 2011, the Estate Tax is scheduled to be reinstated and Estates worth more than $1,000,000 will once again be subject to a sizeable Estate Tax. A couple with an Estate in excess of a million dollars can reduce the risk of an Estate Tax by setting up his and her Trusts, so that each person can take advantage of his own Exclusion Amount.

For example, if a husband and wife own two million dollars, they can separate their funds into two Trusts each valued at one million dollars. The Trusts can be set up so that a surviving spouse can use the income from the deceased partner's Trust for living expenses. In this way, their standard of living need not be reduced by separating their funds into two Trusts.

If they do not wish to separate funds, they can set up a single Joint Trust that separates into two Trusts once one partner dies. Again, the surviving spouse is free to use the income from both Trusts. Once both partners are deceased, the beneficiaries of their respective Trusts will inherit the funds, hopefully with no Estate Tax due.

If the couple makes no Trust provision, and they hold their property jointly, the last to die will own the two million dollars with only one Estate Tax Exclusion available. If lawmakers do not change the tax law, and the surviving spouse dies in 2011, or later, one million dollars of their Estate will be subject to an Estate Tax. A Revocable Living Trust is a relatively simple way for a married couple to reduce, if not eliminate, the need to   pay Estate taxes; however, there is still the problem of the federal Gift Tax and the Capital Gains Tax.

THE UN-UNIFIED GIFT TAX

Up until the year 2002, if you gave someone more than $10,000 in any given year you had to report that gift to the IRS. As explained, the Annual Gift Tax Exclusion is now adjusted for the cost of living and is currently $11,000. The IRS keeps a running count of amounts that you give over the Annual Gift Tax Exclusion. Although you are required to report the gift, no tax need be paid unless that running total is more than the federal Estate Tax Exclusion amount. If your running total does not exceed that amount during your lifetime, once you die, the cumulative value of gifts reported to the IRS will be added to your Taxable Estate.

Until the tax law was changed, the Gift and Estate tax were unified. No Gift Tax needed to be paid unless the total value of the taxable gifts exceeded the federal Estate Tax Exclusion amount. In 2004 that changed. The Estate Tax Exclusion amount went up to $1,500,000, but the amount for the Gift Tax Exclusion remained at $1,000,000, so they now are no longer unified.

To summarize:
If you make a gift to anyone that is greater than the Annual Gift Tax Exclusion for that year, you must report the gift to the IRS. The IRS will keep count of values that you gave in excess of the Annual Gift Tax Exclusion. In 2004, and thereafter, if that sum exceeds $1,000,000, you will pay a Gift Tax on any amount you give that is over the Annual Gift Tax Exclusion.

The Estate Tax is scheduled to be repealed in 2010, but not the Gift Tax.

Virginia does not have a Gift Tax at this time.

The current federal Estate tax is scheduled to be phased out in the year 2010, but a new Capital Gains Tax is scheduled for 2010 that may prove even more costly than the Estate Tax. The new Capital Gains Tax is related to the way inherited property is evaluated by the federal government. Real and personal property is inherited at a "step-up" in basis, meaning that if the decedent's property has increased in value from the time he acquired it, the beneficiary will inherit the property at its fair market value as of the decedent's date of death. For example, if the decedent bought stock for $20,000 and it is worth $50,000 as of his date of death, the beneficiary will take a step-up in basis of $30,000; i.e. the beneficiary inherits the stock at the current $50,000 value. If the beneficiary sells the stock for $50,000, he pays no Capital Gains Tax. If the beneficiary holds onto the stock and later sells it for $60,000, the beneficiary will pay a Capital Gains Tax only on the $10,000 increase in value since the decedent's death.

Up to 2009, there is no limit to the amount a beneficiary can take as a step-up in basis. But in 2010 caps are set in place. The decedent's Estate will be allowed a 1.3 million dollar step-up in basis, plus another 3 million for property passing to the surviving spouse (IRS Code 1022(b)). The new law could result in significant Capital Gains taxes that the beneficiary must pay. For example, suppose in 2010 you inherit a business from your father that he purchased for $100,000 and it is now worth 2 million dollars. There is a capital gain of 1.9 million dollars, but you are allowed a step-up in basis of only 1.3 million. If you sell it for 2 million dollars $600,000 of your inheritance will be subject to a Capital Gains tax.

We will discuss methods of reducing the Gift Tax and the Capital Gains Tax in Chapter 7.

MAYBE A WILL IS BEST AFTER ALL

Although many methods can be used to transfer property without the need for Probate, it may be each method has a downside that is objectionable to you. Maybe you don't have enough money to warrant the cost of setting up the Trust at this time. Holding property jointly with another may raise issues of security and independence. Holding property so that it goes directly to a few beneficiaries in a Pay On Death account may not be as flexible as you wish. This may be the case if you want to give gifts to several charities or to a minor child.

For example, you can hold all your property so that it goes directly to your son without the need for Probate. If you ask him to use some of the money for your grandchild's education, it may be that your grandchild gets none of the money because your son is sued or falls upon hard times. If you keep your property in your name only and leave a Will giving a certain amount of money to your grandchild, the child will know exactly how much money you left and the purpose of that gift.

After taking into account all the pros and cons of avoiding Probate, you may well opt for a Will and a Probate procedure. If you make such a decision, it is important to keep in mind that Estate Planning is not an "all or nothing" choice. You can arrange your Estate so that certain items pass automatically to your intended beneficiary, and other items can be left in your name only, to be distributed as part of a Probate procedure. By arranging your finances in this manner, you can reduce the value of your Probate Estate, and that in turn should reduce the cost of Probate.

In the next chapter, we discuss the Will as an Estate Planning tool.

Those of you who have a Will may be thinking that there is no reason to read the Chapter, but does your Will:

- Make provision for the amount to be paid to your Personal Representative?

- Make gifts of your personal property? (jewelry, car, etc.)

- Name a Guardian to care for your minor child?

- Make adjustment for gifts or loans that you gave to the beneficiaries of your Will?

- Give specific instructions about how your bills and taxes are to be paid; i.e., which of your beneficiaries will have his inheritance reduced in order to pay your debts and taxes?

Has your Will been prepared so that it will be difficult for anyone to challenge it?

Have you stored your Will so that it is safe AND easily accessible to you during your lifetime and to your Personal Representative after your death?

If you answered "Yes" to all of the above questions, then you can skip over to Chapter 5.

Your Will– Your Way   4

Many people decide that the Will is the best route to go but do not act upon it, thinking it unnecessary to prepare a Will until they are very old and about to die. But according to reports published by the National Center for Health Statistics (a division of the U.S. Department of Health and Human Services) 2 of every 10 people who die in any given year are under the age of 60. Twenty percent may seem like a small number until it hits close to home as it did with a young couple.

Alex and Cathy were an old-fashioned couple in a modern world. When they married, they knew they wanted a large family. There was no question that Cathy would stay home and raise the children while Alex went to work. Luckily he did very well as one of the managers of a string of restaurants. Better yet, he enjoyed his work. He loved to cook and would even take over the kitchen when he returned from work. That suited Cathy just fine because she had her hands full raising their three boys.

Cathy couldn't help thinking how lucky they were that morning as she fixed breakfast. A nice house. Healthy, if not rambunctious, boys. All in all, a comfortable marriage. Her only concern that day was the fact that Alex was flying off on a business trip. All this terrorist news made her nervous about flying. Alex reassured her that it was only an hour's flight, and besides he was flying the company plane and not a commercial airliner.

But it was not terrorists that brought down the plane, just a malfunctioning rudder.

THINGS A WILL CAN DO

Though we all agree that one never knows, still people put off making a Will, figuring that if they die before getting around to it, Virginia law will take over and their property will be distributed in the manner that they would have wanted anyway. The problem with that logic is the complexity of Virginia's Laws of Descent. It isn't too hard to figure out who will inherit your property if you are survived by a spouse, child, parent or sibling. But if none of these survive you the ultimate beneficiary of your property may not be the person you would have chosen, had you taken the time to do so.

Others think that it is not necessary to have a Will because they arranged their finances so that all of their property will be inherited without the need for Probate. But money could come into your Estate after your death. This could happen in any number of ways from winning the lottery and dying (of happiness, no doubt) to receiving insurance funds after your death.

For example, if you die in a house fire, the company that insures your home may need to pay for damages done to the property. In such case, the funds will need to be paid to your Estate. A Personal Representative may need to be appointed and the insurance funds distributed according to Virginia law. If you die without a Will, your Estate may be distributed differently than you would have wished. And, as discussed on the next few pages, there are other important reasons to make a Will.

APPOINT PERSONAL REPRESENTATIVE

The Court will give top priority to the person you name as the *Executor* (i.e., Personal Representative) of your Will. If that person is unable or unwilling to serve, or if you die without a Will, the Clerk of the Court can appoint whoever is the main beneficiary of your Estate for the job. If you have more than one beneficiary, they can all sign a waiver appointing someone to serve as Personal Representative. If no one seeks appointment within thirty days of the death, any beneficiary can ask the Clerk to be appointed. If no one is appointed after sixty days from the date of death, anyone (including your creditor) can ask to be Personal Representative of your Estate (VA 64.1-116, 64.1-118).

SET PERSONAL REPRESENTATIVE'S FEE

Once you decide on a Personal Representative, you need to check with that person to be sure that he is willing to serve in that capacity. And if so, you should come to an understanding about how much compensation he will receive to settle your Estate. You can have your attorney make provision for your Personal Representative's compensation in your Will. If you do not do so, under Virginia law, he is entitled to a "reasonable" fee (VA 26-30).

The law does not offer guidelines as to what is reasonable. You might call a few law firms and ask what a Personal Representative is generally paid to settle an Estate equal in value to your current Probate Estate (i.e., property titled in your name only). Once you have an idea of the going rate, you and your Personal Representative can decide on a fee that is mutually agreeable.

CAUTION THE PERSONAL REPRESENTATIVE CAN SEEK MORE MONEY

You can put the amount of agreed compensation in your Will, however your Personal Representative might find it more work than he expected and ask the Court to be given more money. To avoid the problem, you can have your attorney draft an Agreement that you and your Personal Representative sign and then attach to your Will. Having a separate fee Agreement will not stop your Personal Representative from asking for more money, but with such an Agreement, the Court will not agree to the increase unless something unusual occurs (such as a law suit) causing much more work than the ordinary Probate procedure.

You also need to keep in mind that the Personal Representative's fee is just to administer the Estate. It does not include payment for professional work he may do while settling the Estate. For example, if you appoint your attorney as Personal Representative, he can agree to the amount stated in the Will for his role as Personal Representative, and then ask the Court to award him attorney's fees as well.

The same goes for any other professional. If you appoint your accountant to serve as Personal Representative, he is entitled to receive compensation for his work as Personal Representative and also for any accounting work he does such as preparing and filing tax returns, preparing an inventory and doing an accounting for the beneficiaries. A financial planner who serves as Personal Representative may be compensated for his management of the Estate property (buying and selling securities, taking care of rental property, etc.) in addition to his fee to administer the Estate.

But the main problem with appointing a professional as your Personal Representative is the same as appointing a professional to serve as the Successor Trustee of your Trust; namely, that it creates a potential conflict of interest. The professional can use his position as Personal Representative to generate fees that might have been avoided had someone else settled the Estate.

Unless the professional is the sole beneficiary of your Will, it is better to choose a non-professional to settle your Estate.

MAKE GIFTS OF YOUR PERSONAL PROPERTY

Another benefit to making a Will is that you can make provision for who will get your personal property (computers, antiques, securities, boats, snowmobiles etc.). When making a Will consider making provision for your car. If you make a *specific gift* i.e. a gift to a named beneficiary of your Will, it will be relatively simple for your Personal Representative to transfer the car to your beneficiary. If you do not make a specific gift of your car, then your Personal Representative will decide what to do with it. He may decide to sell it and include the proceeds of the sale in the Estate funds to be distributed as part of the Probate Estate; or he can give the car to one beneficiary of your Estate as part of that beneficiary's share of the Estate.

SMALL GIFTS MATTER

Many who have lost someone close to them report that the distribution of small personal items caused the greatest conflict. If you arrange your finances so that Probate procedure is necessary, your next of kin will need to decide among themselves, how to distribute your personal effects. Without guidance from you and no Personal Representative with authority to make decisions, there could be disagreement, and hard feelings, over items of little monetary value but much sentimental value.

If you make a Will, then under Virginia law, you can make gifts of your personal effects (books, music collection, clothing, etc.) by making a list of these gifts and attaching it to your Will. Your Personal Representative will distribute your *personal effects* according to that list. You can change the list at any time just so long as you sign and date the list. No witness to your signature is needed. The list is for items with more sentimental than monetary value. You should not include money gifts, securities or real property in the list. Those items need to be given as part of your Will (VA 64.1-45.1).

Of course, it is not possible to make a list of each and every item you own; but you can instruct your Personal Representative to allow certain family members to take their choice of items not mentioned in your Will. If two or more family members want the same item, instruct your Personal Representative to use an appropriate lottery system (coin toss, high card in a cut of a deck of cards, etc.) to decide who "wins."

YOU CAN'T GIVE WHAT YOU DON'T HAVE

You need to give considerable thought whenever you make a specific gift to someone. It could be that you no longer own the item at the time of your death. This could happen with property or money. For example, suppose you leave all of your Estate to your son, with a specific gift of $10,000 to each of your three grandchildren. Your son is the *residuary beneficiary* of the Probate Estate, meaning he gets whatever is left once all of the bills are paid and all specific gifts distributed. If the cost of your last illness leaves your Probate Estate with only $30,000, would you want the grandchildren to get their gifts and your son nothing? The simple solution is to make all of them residuary beneficiaries by leaving each a percent of your Estate. For example, instead of making a specific gift to each grandchild you could leave 70% to your son and 10% to each grandchild.

NON-PROBATE ASSETS
Property held in a Beneficiary Account, the proceeds of a life insurance policy, Trust property, Joint account with Right of Survivor and IRA accounts are all *Non-probate* assets because they will be inherited by your named beneficiary without the need for Probate. You are free to change the beneficiary during your lifetime, but once you are deceased, the gift is made. You cannot change the beneficiary of such gift in your Will because you have, in effect, already made a gift of that asset. Unless you named your Estate as the beneficiary of a Non-probate asset, it should not even be mentioned in your Will. To do so might cause your Will to be challenged by whoever was named as the beneficiary of the Non-probate asset.

📄   MAKE ADJUSTMENT FOR PRIOR GIFTS

With a Will, you can make adjustments for gifts or loans given during your lifetime. For example, if you have loaned money to a family member and do not expect to be repaid, then you can deduct the loan from that person's inheritance. Of course, it may be that you are not concerned with inequities. That was the case of an aged woman who had three children, Paul, Rita and Frank, her youngest. Frank always seemed to need some assistance from his mother. She often "loaned" him money that he never repaid.

Her other children were responsible and independent. Paul was married and had children of his own. He decided to purchase a house but was having trouble accumulating the down payment. His mother agreed to lend him the money. Paul and his wife offered to give his mother a mortgage on the property. The mother said a simple promissory note from Paul was sufficient, and she would have her attorney draft the note.

The attorney drafted the note but was concerned about the inequity "You never made a Will. Were you to die, each of your children will inherit an equal amount of money. If Paul still owes money on this promissory note, he will either need to pay the balance to your Estate, or have it subtracted from the amount he inherits. All of the money you gave to Frank will not count towards his inheritance unless you make your intentions clear that you considered the money you gave to Frank to be an advancement of his inheritance. You can do this by making an adjustment in a Will, or by having Frank give you a promissory note for any outstanding debts.

"It's O.K." replied the mother "I love all my children equally . . . some are a little more equal than others."

▤ MAKE PROVISION FOR PAYMENT OF DEBTS

Most Wills contain an instruction to the Personal Representative to ". . . pay all the expenses of my last illness, funeral expenses, costs of administration, taxes and just debts. . . " This does not present a problem if you are leaving all of your property to one person. That person will pay all of your bills and keep whatever is left. And there is no problem if you are leaving your Estate equally to several people because whatever is left will be distributed equally to those people. But if you leave a specific gift to someone and you owe money on that item, and do not indicate how the loan should be paid, that could create a major problem.

For example, suppose the mother discussed on the previous page, made a Will leaving everything to her three children, equally, with the exception of her car which she left to Frank. Further suppose, that she owed $10,000 on that car at the time of her death. If her Will did not specify that Frank was to be responsible to pay the monies owed on the car, he might demand that the Estate pay the debt. If his siblings refused to pay, the matter would need to be decided by the Court.

Considering how the mother treated Frank during her lifetime, the Court could well decide that it was her intent to have the $10,000 paid from the Probate Estate. Should the Court order the Estate to pay the loan, there will be $10,000 less for the residuary beneficiaries of the Estate to inherit. That means that Paul and Rita's inheritance will be reduced to pay off the car loan, leaving Frank, as before, a little more "equal" than his siblings.

📑 MAKE PROVISION FOR PAYMENT OF TAXES

Taxes are another concern for those Estates large enough to be subject to Estate Taxes. State and federal law require that Estate Taxes be paid by the beneficiaries of the Estate in proportion to the value received, unless the decedent made some other arrangements to pay for the taxes. If you make no provision for the payment of taxes, whoever inherits your property will pay a percentage of the taxes based on the amount they receive.

The beneficiary must pay his share regardless of whether he inherits the property through a Non-probate transfer (joint owner, beneficiary of your Trust, beneficiary of a Pay On Death account, beneficiary of a life insurance policy, etc.) or as the beneficiary of your Probate Estate. If a beneficiary refuses to contribute his share of the taxes, under Virginia law whoever is required to make payment (usually the surviving spouse or Personal Representative) can ask the Court to order the beneficiary to contribute his share of the taxes (VA 64.1-161).

If this is not as you wish you can direct your Personal Representative to pay all of your taxes from your Probate Estate. If you do so, beneficiaries of a specific gift, and those who inherit property from a Non-probate transfer will not contribute to the payment of your taxes. All of your taxes will be paid from your Probate Estate. This means that the amount that your residuary beneficiaries receive will be reduced by the amount of taxes paid.

▤ CHOOSE A GUARDIAN FOR YOUR MINOR CHILD

If one parent dies, then it is the right, and duty, of the surviving parent to care for the child. But it could happen that both parents become incapacitated or die before the child is grown. If you have a minor child, you can use your Will to appoint someone to serve as the child's Guardian in the event that the other parent is deceased or incapacitated. You can name someone to serve as Guardian of property that you leave for your child. Better yet, you can include a Trust in your Will, naming someone to serve as Trustee to care for property left to the child under your Will (VA 31-1, 31-2).

See Chapter 7 for more information about how to make provision for the care of your minor child in the event of your incapacity or death.

After reading the past few pages you may think "Looks like everyone should have a Will." And we would agree with your conclusion. Regardless of whether you arrange for all of your property to pass directly without the need for Probate; and regardless of whether you have a Trust, it is important that you have a Will for all of the reasons just stated.

In Virginia, you can prepare a Will without the assistance of an attorney. In fact you don't even need a witness to your Will. You can sit down write one out yourself. Such a Will is called a *holographic* Will. Many states have laws prohibiting the Court from accepting a holographic Will. In Virginia, a holographic Will can be admitted into Probate, provided you write it all in your own hand, and two independent, disinterested persons testify to the Court that they recognize the handwriting as yours (VA 64.1-49).

That may sound like a simple thing, however, if the Will is contested, each opposing party will, no doubt, be able to find two expert witness who support their position.

Having two people witness you signing your Will can head off the problem of whether you made the Will; however, if either witness is a beneficiary of your Will, someone may accuse the witness of pressuring you into giving the gift. Under Virginia law just the fact that the witness to your Will is also a beneficiary of your Will does not automatically make the Will or the gift invalid (VA 8.01-396, 64.1-51). But someone could challenge your Will saying that the beneficiary of the gift used *undue influence* to make you give them a gift.

Undue influence is not easily proved. Virginia courts have ruled that whoever is saying that undue influence was used must prove that the Will maker had no free will, and that someone was controlling his mind and action when he made his Will (*Pace v. Richmond*, 2321 Va 216 (1986), 343 S.E.2d 59). But just because it may be hard to prove undue influence, it does not mean that it can't be done, nor that some family member will be discouraged from challenging your Will because of the difficulty.

And your Will can be challenged on other grounds.

A Will needs to be worded clearly and in conformance with Virginia law. There may be a dispute as to the meaning of a Will if a sentence can be read in two ways. Even if your Will is clearly worded, properly signed and witnessed, it can still be challenged if you are married and did not make proper provision for your spouse. As explained on page 51, your spouse has the right to an Elective Share unless he/she signed a valid prenuptial or postnuptial agreement giving up that right (VA 64.1-13). Your spouse has the right to demand the amount allowed by law, if you do not make provision in your Will for at least one third of your Estate to go to your spouse.

Although your spouse has the right to elect against your Will, your adult child has no such statutory right. You can give your child as much, or as little as you wish. You have the right to give the child nothing at all.

If you are concerned that someone may challenge your Will, it is important that you consult with an attorney who is experienced in Estate Planning. The attorney will prepare the Will according to your wishes. If you meet with the attorney in the privacy of his office, and without anyone else present, it will be difficult to prove that someone was using undue influence to make you make gifts according to their wishes and not yours.

Once the Will is prepared according to your direction, the attorney can supervise the signing of your Will. He will see to it that your Will is signed and witnessed in the presence of two disinterested witnesses — usually members of his staff. Signing the Will in this manner is protection against a challenge. Your attorney will be able to present proof to the Court that the Will was prepared exactly as you wished, and that no one was present to influence you. The attorney and the witnesses to your Will, can testify that you signed the Will willingly and that you were competent to know what you were doing when you signed the Will.

You can even have your attorney include a *no contest* provision in your Will stating that if a beneficiary named in your Will challenges any provision in the Will, then he will inherit none of your Probate Estate. Such a provision is called an *In Terrorem Clause* because it is designed to cause fear (if not terror) in the heart of your beneficiary. Many states will not enforce such a clause, because they want people to have the right to challenge a Will, and then let the Court decide whether that challenge is proper.

Virginia Courts have enforced an In Terrorem Clause where it was determined that the Will was valid (*Womble v. Gunter*, 198 Va. 522 (1956), 95 S.E.2d 213). This does not mean that all In Terrorem Clauses are automatically enforced in the state of Virginia. The Court could find that the Will was not valid and there was *probable cause* ** for the challenge. For example, if the Court finds that the Will was a forgery, or is not valid for some other reason, then whoever made the challenge will not be barred from inheriting your Estate because of that provision in the Will.

** Lawyer talk for "had a good reason to do so"

STORING YOUR WILL

Once you sign your Will, you may wonder where to store it. If an attorney prepared your Will, he may suggest that he place it in his vault for safekeeping. By doing so, he ensures that your heirs will need to contact him as soon as you die. This does not mean that they are required to employ him should a Probate procedure be necessary. It only means that he will have an opportunity for future employment.

But there are problems with such an arrangement. The Will could be lost or mistaken for another Will. That happened in at least one case. The attorney prepared Wills for two people with the same name and similar family circumstances. When one person died the attorney submitted the wrong Will to Probate.

If you decide to allow your attorney to store the Will, you need assurance that the attorney will be responsible for the document. You should get a receipt and something in writing that says:

⇨   The attorney accepts full responsibility for storage of the Will. Should it be lost or damaged, he will replace the document at no cost to you; and if you are deceased, he will, at no cost to your heirs, present sufficient evidence to the Court to accept a valid copy of the Will into Probate.

⇨   There will be no charge to you, or your heirs, for the storage and retrieval of the document.

⇨   Should he sell his practice, retire, or die, he or the successor to his practice, will return the original document to you.

THE SAFE DEPOSIT BOX, SAFE BUT . . .

You might consider placing your document in a safe deposit box that you lease at a bank. The only problem with the bank safe deposit box is convenient access. In Virginia, if you hold a safe deposit box in your name only, access to the box is restricted once you die. Your next of kin can ask the bank to let them inspect the box to see if a Will is in the box. Under Virginia law, the bank may allow the spouse or next of kin to look at the contents of the box under the supervision of an officer or employee of the company. If the Will is there, the family member or bank can arrange to have it delivered to the Clerk of the Circuit Court.

Other than the Will, nothing else can be removed from the safe deposit box without authorization from the Clerk (VA 6.1-332.1). That authorization may need to be in the form of Letters granted to the person appointed as your Personal Representative.

For those who are married, the solution to the problem of accessing the safe deposit box after death, is to lease the box jointly with your spouse, such that each of you has free access to the box. Those who have a Trust can solve the problem by giving their Successor Trustee joint access to the safe deposit box.

If you are single and do not have a Trust, you can lease the box jointly with a trusted family member. If you both have free access to the box, the surviving joint renter can go to the box and remove all of its contents (VA 6.1-332).

Of course, if privacy and security are important to you, that may outweigh any concern for the convenience of your beneficiaries.

STORE IT WITH THE COURT

Perhaps the best place to store your Will is with the Probate Court in the county of your residence. Virginia law gives residents the right to deposit their Will with the Clerk of the Probate Court. The only problem is that the law does not require all Courts to do so. The judge of the Probate Court can enter an order authorizing the Clerk to use his office to store Wills for the residents of that county, or not.

If you live in a county that accepts Wills, you can deposit it for a fee of $2. You are free to retrieve the Will from the Clerk in the event that you move or decide to change your Will. Once you are deceased, the Clerk will deliver the Will to the person you named as Executor (VA 64.1-56).

Regardless of where you choose to store your Will, let your Personal Representative know that you have a Will and how to retrieve it in the event of your death.

A Will is Not Enough in Virginia

I thought you said a Will is not enough

After reading this chapter, you may be thinking that the book is poorly named. After all, look at all the good things a Will can do:

* choose the person you want to settle your Estate
* arrange to have your Personal Representative settle your Estate for a reasonable fee
* give your personal items, including your car, to the person of your choice
* choose a Guardian for your child
* discourage a challenge to your Will.

But that is not all there is to an Estate Plan. A Will cares for your property when you are deceased, but it cannot provide for the care of your property in the event you become disabled. A complete Estate Plan provides for the care of your property during your lifetime and for the care of your person as well.

In these days of extended old age, many of us will need assistance with our health care and/or finances as we age. It is important to arrange to have someone manage finances and make medical decisions in the event that we are too aged or too ill to do so ourselves. These topics are covered in Chapters 8 and 9.

And a Will may be effective to transfer all that you own upon your death, but it cannot help your family pay for your debts. It may be that you have so many debts that your family is left with little or nothing. A complete Estate Plan provides for the financial well being of your family once you are deceased; and that is the topic of the next chapter.

Arranging To Pay Bills 5

You can think of your Estate Plan as being composed of two separate parts, a Lifetime Plan and an Inheritance Plan. Your Lifetime Plan provides for the care of your property during your lifetime, with the goal being maximum control and protection. Your Inheritance Plan provides for the inheritance of your property, with the goal being minimum cost and hassle to your beneficiaries. You could consider your Estate Plan to be a master plan that balances the goals of the Lifetime Plan with those of the Inheritance Plan.

When people consider their Inheritance Plan, they are mostly concerned about giving their possessions away. Many do not take into account how the bills they have accumulated will be paid once they are deceased, or even who will be responsible for paying those bills. Most of us do not worry about providing for the payment of our debts, thinking "I'll have that paid off long before I die." But with easily available credit, many are maintaining a high debt balance as a way of life. Paying off all of their loans is not a priority. Many will live their lives without ever being free of debt.

This does not imply that people do not know how to manage their funds. For many people (and corporations), it makes good sense to use other people's money to carry on business. In fact, great debt is a badge of honor for the wealthy. If a bank will lend you a million dollars, it means you have the means to repay that amount. Banks will not lend much money to those with few assets. Rich or poor, we all need to think about how our debts will be paid once we are gone.

WHO IS RESPONSIBLE TO PAY BILLS?

Suppose you die without funds, and owing money. Does the debt die with you or is someone else responsible to pay what you owe? If you are married, the first person the creditor will look to, is your spouse. To understand the basis of this expectation, you need to know a bit of the history of our legal system.

Our laws are derived from the English Common Law. Under English Common law, a single woman had the right to own property in her own name and also the right to contract to buy or sell property. When a woman married, her legal identity merged with her spouse. She could not hold property free from her husband's claim or control. She could no longer enter into a contract without her husband's permission.

Once married, a woman became financially dependent on her husband. He, in turn, became legally responsible to provide his wife with basic necessities — food, clothing, shelter and medical services. If anyone provided basic necessities to his wife, then, regardless of whether the husband agreed to be responsible for the debt, he became obliged to pay for them. This law was called the DOCTRINE OF NECESSARIES.

In the United States, a series of Married Women's Rights Acts were passed giving a married woman the right to own property. Married woman have had the right to own property in Virginia since April 4, 1877 (VA 55-35).

As Married Women's Rights laws were passed state to state, a series of cases tested whether the Doctrine of Necessaries still applied in that state.

Questions that judges had to decide were:

If a wife can own property and contract to pay for her own necessities, should her husband be responsible for such debts in the event she does not have enough money to pay for them?

And if the husband is responsible to pay for his wife's necessities should she be responsible for his?

In some states, notably Florida, courts decided that neither partner was responsible to pay the other's necessities, unless they contracted or agreed to do so. In Virginia, the Supreme Court refused to rule on the issue saying that it was something the legislature should decide (*Schilling v. Bedford Co. Hospital*, 225 Va. 539 (1983), 303 S.E.2d 905).

The Virginia legislature responded to the invitation and expanded the Doctrine so that each partner is responsible to pay for necessities. The current law in Virginia requires that if the spouse who made the contract or purchase, does not have sufficient funds to pay for the necessities, then his/her spouse is equally liable for the debt. The non-contracting spouse is not liable for the necessities if the couple is permanently separated. Other than for necessities, neither spouse is responsible to pay for the other's debts unless they both agreed to be liable (VA 55-37).

Which leads to the next question. Is anyone other than your spouse responsible to pay monies you owe?

For joint debts, the answer is "yes."

JOINT DEBTS

A *joint debt* is a debt that two or more people are responsible to pay. Usually the contract or promissory note reads that both parties agree to *joint and several* liability, meaning they both agree to pay the debt and each of them, individually, agrees to pay the debt. A joint debt can also be in the form of monies owed by one person with payment guaranteed by another person. If the person who owes the money does not pay, the *guarantor* (the person who guaranteed payment) is responsible to pay the debt.

Should you die, your hospital bills, nursing home bills, funeral expenses, legal fees for the Probate of your Estate, are all debts of your Estate. They are not joint debts unless someone guaranteed payment for the monies owed. Hospital and nursing home bills are considered to be necessaries, so if you are married and there are insufficient funds in the Estate to pay for these bills, then your spouse is responsible for payment, regardless of whether your spouse agreed to be jointly liable for the debt.

JOINT SPOUSAL DEBTS

A surviving spouse may need to pay for the decedent's necessaries, but not for any other debt unless the debt was joint (VA 55-37). Your spouse is responsible to pay for loans signed by both of you. For example, if you both are authorized to use a credit card, and there is no money in your Estate, then your spouse is responsible to pay the debt. Property taxes are a joint debt if you and your spouse both own the property.

JOINT PROPERTY BUT NO JOINT DEBT

Suppose you have a credit card in your name only, and you have a joint bank account with your son. Should you die, can the credit card company require that half of the joint funds be set aside to pay the debt? In Virginia, the answer is "yes," but with some restrictions. The Personal Representative is under no duty to ask for the monies in the joint account, but if there is not enough money in your Probate Estate to pay off your credit card, and the credit card company writes to your Personal Representative asking that your half of the joint account be used to pay your debt, then the Personal Representative will ask the financial institution to freeze the account and not distribute the monies until the matter is settled by the Probate Court. The written demand must be made within six months from the date the Personal Representative is appointed. If that demand is not made within that time, whoever is entitled to the decedent's share of the account is free to keep it (VA 64.1-140).

BUT NOT EXEMPT FROM UNCLE SAM

The surviving joint owner of an account has no obligation to use the joint account funds to pay your creditors unless a claim is made on the account within six months. However, your share of the joint account is included as part of your Taxable Estate. If Estate Taxes are due, the beneficiary of your share of the account needs to pay any part of that tax that is due because of the monies he inherited. The beneficiary will not need to pay his share of the Estate Taxes if you make some other provision for the payment of your taxes. For example, you can give instructions in your Will or Trust that all your taxes are to be paid from your Probate Estate or from monies you set aside for that purpose (VA 64.1-160, 64.1-161, 64.1-165).

You may be wondering what happens if the surviving owner of the joint account takes out the money from the account before the credit card company gets a chance to ask for the money. In such case, the Probate Court can require that the surviving joint owner pay your share of the joint bank account to the credit card company.

A similar situation occurs if you are holding monies in a Pay On Death bank account with instructions to the bank to give the money to your son once you die. Should you die the bank will give the money in the account to your son, but if that money is needed to pay your debts, your Personal Representative can ask your son to pay as much money from the account as needed to pay the debt.

There is a six month Statute of Limitations for a joint account, but there is a two year statute of limits on a Pay On Death account, so your creditors have two years from the date of death to ask for the monies in that account (VA 6.1-125.8, 6.1-125.11)

PAYING FOR CREDIT CARD DEBT

As discussed, if you hold a credit card jointly with another, you are both equally liable to pay that debt. Should one of you die, the other is responsible to pay the bill regardless of who ran up the bill. If paying that bill could be a struggle for the surviving debtor, you might consider credit card insurance to cover the debt. Most credit card companies offer insurance policies and include the premium as part of the monthly payment. It benefits the credit card company to offer life insurance as part of the credit package, because they are assured of prompt payment should the borrower die.

If you are married and hold a credit card jointly with your spouse, you might consider purchasing credit card insurance. Of course, in these days of exorbitant credit card interest rates, you may be struggling to pay your monthly charge. Adding still another charge to the account may not be an option, regardless of the security offered to your spouse. In such case, a better route might be for you to remove your name from the account and open a new account in your name only. Your surviving spouse will not be responsible to pay your credit card debts, unless the items you charged were for basic necessities (food, clothing, shelter).

Still another reason not to hold a joint credit card is that each of you can establish your own line of credit. This is especially important if you are married and one of you is retired or has been out of the job market for any period of time. Should the breadwinner die, it may be difficult for the surviving partner to establish credit if he/she has no recent work record. It is easier for the unemployed spouse to establish a line of credit when he/she is married to someone who is working.

OTHER TYPES OF LOAN INSURANCE

Many mortgage companies offer mortgage insurance to their borrowers. Mortgage rates are currently low, so an additional charge for mortgage insurance on the life of the primary wage earner may be worth the effort. This is particularly the case with families raising children. With such insurance, the family can inherit the homestead free of debt. The monthly insurance charge may be a small price to pay to ensure that the children can continue to live in their own home until they are grown.

Car loan insurance is still another thing to consider. If a married couple purchases (or leases) a car, and one of them dies, it may be a struggle for the other to pay off the loan. This was the case with Eva and Howard. Both had to work to support their three children. They owned two well used cars. It seemed that one car or the other was always in the shop. When they saw a **NO INTEREST** advertisement for a new car, they decided the offer was too good to pass up.

The monthly payments were high, but it was their only luxury. With both their salaries, they were able to make the payments. When Howard had his first heart attack, he was out of work for several weeks so they struggled to keep the payments current. Howard worked in construction, and was anxious to return to work. The doctors advised that such work might be too strenuous for his weakened heart. Construction work was all Howard knew, and the pay was good, so he ignored the warning and went back to his old job.

The second heart attack was fatal, leaving Eva as the sole means of support for her family.

With Howard gone there was no need for two cars. Eva could not afford the payments on the new car anyway, so she decided to sell it. Unfortunately, what she could get for the car was significantly less than the balance owed. Once she fell behind in payments she decided to surrender the car rather than have them repossess it. She was sure they would understand, considering all that she had been through these past several months, not to mention that she was a widow with three small children.

They didn't understand.

The company took the car and then sued for the balance of monies owed. The judge was sympathetic, but under the law there is no "life is tough" defense. He ruled that Eva had to pay the monies owed; and, as per the terms of the loan agreement, she even had to pay the fees for the company's attorney and all court costs. What an emotional and financial nightmare!

The pity was, it all could have been avoided, had they worked payment of debts into their Estate Plan. Howard was the primary driver of the new car and the primary wage earner. All he had to do was put the loan in his name only, and take out loan insurance. Eva would have inherited the car, debt free. She could have kept it or sold it as she saw fit.

Even if Howard didn't purchase loan insurance, had he put the loan in his name only, the company could only have sued his Estate. They would not have been able to sue Eva personally.

PURCHASING LIFE INSURANCE

The good part of purchasing loan insurance — be it credit card insurance, mortgage insurance or car insurance, is that you can usually purchase the insurance without taking a medical examination. The down side is that companies generally do not offer such insurance to those over the age of 65; and for those under 65 the cost of the insurance is a factor. It usually costs more to purchase loan insurance than a life insurance policy. Those in fairly good health need to comparison shop. If it is your goal to have insurance cover all of your outstanding debts, then the cost of a single life insurance policy may be much less than purchasing several loan insurance policies.

The Estate Planning strategy of purchasing life insurance to pay off all of your loans works best if you are married and your spouse is jointly liable for your debts. If you name your spouse as beneficiary of the life insurance policy, he/she can use the life insurance funds to pay off all monies owed. If you name your spouse (or anyone else) as beneficiary of your insurance policy, and that person has no legal obligation to pay your debts, then none of your creditors can ask your beneficiary to use the insurance funds to pay your debts (VA 38.2-3122).

If you want the insurance funds used to pay your debts, then this may not be the way to go. But, if you want to be sure that someone receives money for their care after you are gone, and you do not want those funds reduced by the cost of Probate or to pay off your debts, then this strategy should accomplish your goal.

With or without debt, you may be wondering about life insurance — should you have it? How much is enough? The answer to these questions depends on the "sleep at night" factor, namely how much insurance do you need so that you won't worry about insurance coverage when you go to sleep at night? It is often more an emotional than a financial issue.

Some people have an "every man for himself" attitude and are content to have no life insurance at all. When they die, whatever they have, they have. And that is what their heirs will inherit. Others worry about how their loved ones will manage if they are not around to support them, and decide to purchase enough insurance to maintain their dependents in their accustomed life style.

The same person may have different thoughts about insurance coverage as circumstances change — from no coverage in his bachelor days to more-than-enough coverage in his child rearing days to just-enough-to-bury-me in his senior years.

Insurance companies recognize that people's needs change over the years. Many companies offer flexible insurance coverage. As with any consumer item, it is a good idea to shop around. In addition to the problem of how much life insurance to carry, there is the concern of how the monies will be spent. Leaving a large sum of money to a person who is less than prudent, may lead to a spending spree.

Most beneficiaries go through their inheritance within two years. For many, the reason the money is gone so soon, is that there just wasn't much money to inherit in the first place. But for others, it's a spending frenzy. Luckily, people are fairly consistent in their spending habits, so you probably know in advance whether your intended beneficiary will "go wild," or prudently invest the monies he inherits.

If you want to leave an insurance policy benefit to someone you love, but the intended beneficiary is immature, or a born spendthrift, then a simple solution to the problem may be to purchase an *Annuity* rather than a life insurance policy with a single lump sum payment. You can purchase an Annuity from an insurance company so that upon your death the *Annuitant*, receives money on a regular basis (monthly, quarterly, yearly) rather than one large payment.

You can even set up the annuity so that it is protected from the creditors of the beneficiary. Virginia law allows up to one million dollars to be so protected (VA 55-19). For example, suppose you purchase an annuity worth $50,000, to be paid at the rate of $1,000 a month to your son. His creditors cannot force the policy to be liquidated to pay monies he owes. Of course once your son takes possession of his monthly payment, then those monies become available to pay his debts.

Up to $1,000,000 of an Annuity is protected from the creditors of the Annuitant. There is unlimited protection from the claims of your creditors. This means that even if you die without money and lots of debt, your creditors will not have access to that Annuity. The Annuity is creditor proof and so are the following items:

✧ LIFE INSURANCE PROCEEDS ✧

As discussed, the beneficiary of your life insurance policy takes the proceeds free of your debts and this is so regardless of the value of the insurance policy. The only exception is the purchase of a policy to defraud creditors. For example, suppose you owe a large sum of money and instead of paying the debt, you use that money to buy a life insurance policy. If the creditor can prove that the purpose of the purchase was to avoid paying the debt, the money you paid for the policy, plus interest on that money, must be paid to the creditors from the proceeds of the policy (VA 38.2-3122).

✧ PREPAID TUITION ✧

Prepaid tuition contracts in the state of Virginia are creditor proof. If you purchase a prepaid tuition contract for your child or grandchild, then your beneficiary is entitled to the proceeds of the contract free of the claims of your creditors (VA 23-38.81).

✧ PENSION PLANS ✧

Annuities, pensions, profit sharing or other retirement plans regulated by the federal Employee Retirement Income Security Act of 1974 ("ERISA"), including IRA accounts and plans identified by the Internal Revenue Code as 401 and 403(a & b), 408, 408A, 409 (as 409 was in effect prior to its repeal) and 457 are creditor proof. Monies received by a beneficiary of such plans are protected from your creditors with some qualifications:

EXEMPTION LIMITED TO $17,500 PER YEAR

There is a limit on the amount of the monies that are exempt from creditors. The amount exempted can be no greater than is necessary to pay the beneficiary $17,500 per year for life. The amount exempted depends on the life expectancy of the beneficiary at the time the exemption is claimed. For example, if the beneficiary is 60 years old, up to $89,512.50 of your retirement is protected from your creditors. Virginia statute 34-34 has an actuary table that you can use to figure out how much of your pension is protected. You will have no trouble using the table if you are very, very, good at math. The rest of us will need the assistance of an accountant or an attorney.

NO EXEMPTION FOR TAXES

In general, income taxes are not paid when money is placed in a retirement plan. Taxes are paid when the monies are withdrawn from the account regardless of whether the monies are withdrawn by the retiree or the person he named as beneficiary of the retirement plan.

Should you die while a resident of Virginia, leaving a spouse and/or minor children, they have certain rights that must be satisfied before any of your creditors can be paid:

FAMILY ALLOWANCE

If Probate is necessary, your spouse and minor child are entitled to receive money for their maintenance while Probate is being conducted. This maintenance is called a *Family Allowance*. The allowance can be paid in periodic installments up to $1,000 per month, or in a single lum sum, up to $12,000 per year. The money is paid to the surviving spouse, but if the minor child does not live with the spouse, the allowance is paid to the child's custodian. The Family Allowance cannot be paid for more than a year if there is not enough money in your Estate to pay for all of the valid *claims* (demands for payment) against your Estate.

The Family Allowance is given in addition to any benefit that the spouse or child may receive from your Estate (VA 64.1-151.1, 64.1-151.4).

EXEMPT PROPERTY

In addition to the Family Allowance, the surviving spouse may keep the household furniture, personal effects, furnishings, appliances, and automobiles, up to a total value of $10,000, not including monies owed on any of the items. If there is no surviving spouse, then your minor child is entitled to keep this *Exempt Property*. If you leave more than one minor child, they will share the Exempt Property, equally (VA 64.1-151.2).

✧ THE HOMESTEAD ALLOWANCE ✧

In addition to the Family Allowance and Exempt Property, the surviving spouse is entitled to a *Homestead Allowance* in the amount of $10,000. If there is no surviving spouse, the decedent's minor children are entitled to the Homestead Allowance which they will share equally. The Homestead Allowance is paid after the Family Allowance is paid and the Exempt Property distributed.

The Homestead Allowance has priority over any creditor, but if the spouse or child decides to take the Homestead Allowance, they will not be able to inherit anything else from the decedent's Estate. If there is not enough money in the Estate to pay all your debts, your spouse (or child) will at least inherit the $10,000.

If there are sufficient monies available to pay all debts, the spouse or child will probably do better to not take their Homestead Allowance, but rather take their share of the inheritance (VA 64.1-151.3).

AN ESTATE PLAN FOR THE BANKRUPT

You may think the above title to be an oxymoron (a contradiction in terms). If a person is bankrupt, why plan for an Estate he doesn't have? But facts are, that people who file for bankruptcy are often quite wealthy and that is their downfall. Because they have substantial income or property, banks and people are willing to lend them money. If more money is borrowed than can be repaid, the unhappy result is bankruptcy. In the event you are concerned about meeting your responsibilities as parent or spouse, yet you enjoy a life style of financial brinksmanship, then consider investing in items that are "creditor proof."

That's exactly what Alan decided to do. Alan was astute, well aware of his strengths and weaknesses. He enjoyed his work and knew he had the capacity to earn large sums of money. But he also knew he was a gambler. Not the Las Vegas type, but a gambler in business ventures. "No risk, no gain" was one his favorite sayings.

If you charted Alan's net worth over the years it would look like the peaks and valleys of the NASDAQ. Lots of high highs and low lows. Unfortunately, he married a woman who did not share his adventurous spirit. His wife became increasingly intolerant of their financial instability. She came to realize that this was his life style and things would never change. "All gamblers die broke," she said as she walked out the door with their 5 year old daughter in tow.

That, and the fact that he had to declare bankruptcy, brought Alan up short; and he began to be concerned about his future and that of his family.

Alan talked things over with his bankruptcy attorney "I am a good businessman, but not a clairvoyant. There was no way to predict the turn of events that led to this situation. But I know I will bounce back, and it will just be a matter of time before I earn my next fortune. I also know that I am an entrepreneur and not a 9 to 5 type guy so this could happen again. What concerns me is how to provide some security for my child in case something happens to me before she is grown." His attorney's response was a surprise: "Move to another state."

"You're kidding."

"Not really. There are few items in Virginia that are creditor proof. Many states have homestead creditor protection, so at least you can keep a roof over your head. A homestead in Texas or Florida is protected 100%, even if it is worth a million dollars. We have minimal protection here in Virginia — $5,000 plus $500 for each of your dependents. If you are a Veteran, you are entitled to another $2,000 exemption. But the Homestead Exemption does not apply to mortgages on your property, or money you owe for spousal or child support (VA 34-4, 34-4.1, 34-5). Your creditors could force the sale of your home to pay for a relatively small amount of money that you owe.

You could put money into a federal retirement plan such as an IRA or Keogh account, and your daughter would inherit that free of your debts."

Alan didn't think that would work. "I am my own boss, and I don't have the self discipline to put money aside each month for my retirement."

The attorney suggested "You can purchase a life insurance policy with your wife or daughter as beneficiary. Regardless of the value of the policy, they would inherit the proceeds free of your debts. The only problem is that the cash value of your policy is available to your creditors during your lifetime."

Alan was annoyed "What about all those millionaires who protect their money in Offshore Trusts? If I really hit it big, why can't I do that?"

"You could, but there are many drawbacks. Just to set up an Offshore Trust costs tens of thousands of dollars, not to mention how much it would cost just to maintain the Trust."

Alan said "Yes, but if I had millions of dollars that would not be a problem."

"True, but there are other considerations. Once you put your money into the Trust, you are essentially giving up control of that money."

Alan was skeptical "Oh come now. Why would anyone put his money where he can't get to it?"

The attorney explained "The Trust can be set up so that funds are available for whatever the millionaire wants. Usually funds are made available to support his family. Trust funds can be used to maintain the family home or yacht. Monies from the Trust can be used to pay for travel or for an expensive vacation. And of course the Trust would provide for the transfer of the property to the millionaire's beneficiaries, once the millionaire dies.

What the millionaire can't do is be the Trustee of the Trust, because if he were, he would have control over the money, and his creditors could take legal action here in the United States to force him to use his Trustee powers to use that money to pay his creditors."

"How can they force the issue? Why couldn't he, as Trustee, just refuse?"

"Remember, that as long as the millionaire is a citizen of the United States, and he is physically present in the states, he is subject to the laws of this country. If a creditor goes to Court and wins, the U. S. Judge could order the millionaire, as Trustee, to use Trust funds to pay that debt. If the millionaire-Trustee refused, the Judge could put him in jail for contempt of Court. No, for an Offshore Trust to work, the Trust must be a foreign Trust, that is, drafted according to the laws of a foreign country, Trust property must be located outside of the United States, and the Trustee cannot be a citizen of the United States."

Alan said "Well I guess the millionaire might have a relative who is not a U.S. citizen to manage the Trust."

The attorney agreed "Yes, or he could use a financial institution that does not do business in the U.S., to manage the funds. But there are other problems with an Offshore Trust. There's the safety factor. Trust funds are kept outside of the United States. If the funds are kept in a foreign bank and the country suffers an economic collapse, then those funds could be lost."

Alan wondered "Isn't that much the same risk as money in a U.S. bank? Only $100,000 of the cash in a U. S. bank account is insured. If the bank fails, any money in that bank over $100,000 could be lost."

The attorney disagreed "Our U.S government is stable, and we trust that they will regulate U.S. banks and keep our money safe. But that is not the case with other small countries. The government of a small country could collapse and the banks along with it."

"But why keep money in a bank? Most millionaires have their funds invested in stocks and bonds, or in real property."

The attorney agreed "True, but real estate could be risky. If your Trust contains real property located within the United States, your creditor could go to a U.S. court and take that property."

Alan wondered "Couldn't the creditor take the overseas property as well?"

"He could, but it would be hard. For one thing he would need to find the property. Even if the creditor locates Trust property, whether it is stocks, bonds, or real estate, most Offshore Trusts are established in countries that are not creditor friendly. For example, if you set up an Off shore Trust in the Cook Islands, they will not accept a judgment that a creditor got in the United States. The creditor will need to employ a Cook Islands attorney to sue you all over again in the Cook Islands. That's expensive. And the Cook Islands have a higher standard of proof. Here in the U.S., all your creditor needs to do is show that you owe the money *by a preponderance of the evidence*. That's lawyer talk for "the jury must be more than 50% sure you owe the money." In the Cook Islands, the creditor's attorney must prove you owe the money *beyond a reasonable doubt* (Cook Islands, International Trusts Act of 1984 Section 13B(1)). In addition, the foreign country usually has a short Statute of Limitations, so if your creditor does not sue within that period of time, he cannot sue you at all."

Alan said "I can see why Offshore Trusts are so popular."

The attorney cautioned "But there are other problems. The U.S. considers transfers into and/or out of the Trust to be taxable. The IRS requires special tax returns to be filed for all foreign Trusts. In addition, the IRS looks closely at Offshore Trusts to determine whether they are fraudulent transfers, designed to avoid U.S. income taxes or U.S. Estate taxes. The IRS wants to be sure that the creditor the millionaire is avoiding isn't Uncle Sam!"

Alan said "Yes, but if you pay your taxes, that shouldn't be a problem. If I ever get to the point where I am that wealthy, I'll come back to discuss setting up an Offshore Trust."

The attorney refused "No, I'm just a country lawyer. If you want to go that route, you need a specialist — someone who has overseas connections, and who has experience in writing such Trusts. If you are serious about setting up an Offshore Trust, let me know and I will recommend someone to you."

"O.K. I will."

The attorney offered a final word of caution "If you are able to accumulate a significant amount of money, don't risk it all in a business venture. Limit the amount of money you can lose to just the money that you invest in business. Keep your personal funds separate and protected from your business debts. If you want to start a business, make sure that you cannot be personally liable for business debts. You can avoid personal liability by forming a corporation, or a Limited Partnership, or a Limited Liability Company.** Stay away from a sole proprietorship or a business partnership."

** These topics are discussed in the next chapter.

Your Business Estate Plan 6

It would take a very thick book to do justice to the topic of Business Estate Planning. Estate Planning issues must be discussed for each type of business:

CONTROL   How to control and protect your business during your lifetime.

BENEFICIARY How to be sure your business goes to the beneficiary of your choice.

COST   How to transfer your business to your beneficiary quickly and at lowest cost.

With just one chapter to devote to the topic, we can only provide the reader with an overview of the subject. Hopefully, the overview will give the reader some ideas that can later be pursued with a financial planner, or an attorney.

We have written this chapter for the reader who listed a business value as part of his Net Worth on page 4. People who are self employed, but who do not think of themselves as business owners, may profit from the information covered in this chapter, as well.

This chapter should also be of interest to someone who has the possibility of inheriting a business interest, such as the child of a small business owner, or perhaps the spouse of someone who is self employed. Even those who are thinking of starting a business, may find it worthwhile to take a few minutes to read this chapter.

Those who have no present business interest may want to skip this chapter and go on to Chapter 7.

TRANSFERRING THE FAMILY BUSINESS

Your business is your property, and as such it is included as part of your overall Estate Plan. But owning a business isn't as simple as just holding title to a tangible item such as a car or parcel of real estate. For example, if you own a business in your name only, i.e. as a *sole proprietor*, there may be no single document that indicates ownership of your business property. You could own a truck, computer, copier or other expensive business equipment. Title to that property is probably in your personal name.

Your business bank account may be in your name only, or in the name of your business with you alone as signatory on the account. Charge cards and business loans are either in your name only, or in your business name with your name as guarantor.

If you want to leave your business to your son, how do you do it? Do you leave him the equipment used in the business? If you are doing business under your own name and not a registered trade name, how do you give him that name? And how do you handle business related loans? If you leave him the business, will he agree to be responsible for any outstanding business debt?

Partnerships can be even more complicated, unless there is a written partnership agreement that says how the business is to be transferred in the event that one of the partners dies. Even the transfer of a corporation can be a major headache if there are several shareholders and no shareholders' agreement to say how shares should be transferred in the event of the death or incapacity of the shareholder.

For these reasons, it is important to think about an Estate Plan for your business. You need to ask yourself:

How can I have maximum protection and control over my business during my lifetime?

How can I structure my business so that it can be transferred quickly and at minimum cost?

We will examine each type of business ownership as it relates to the above questions.

Those who read the first five chapters know us well enough not to expect a definitive answer to the above question. Our job, as we see it, is to explain the rules of the game (i.e., Virginia law) to the reader. Once you know how things work in Virginia, you can make an informed decision as to the type of business ownership that best accomplishes your goal.

SOLE PROPRIETORSHIP
Maximum control — Maximum liability

You are the boss if you do business in your name only, but you take full personal responsibility for any loss suffered by the company; and as explained, you may need to consult with an attorney if you want to make arrangements for someone to take over your business should you become incapacitated or die.

Because of this personal liability issue, many people think it best to form a corporation as soon as they start up the business. That may not be the best strategy. It takes money to form a corporation. You may need to pay an attorney to set up the corporation. You will need to pay to file a Certificate of Incorporation. Each year you need to file an annual report with the State Corporation Commission; and pay an annual Registration fee of $25 or more depending on the number of shares in the company (VA 13.1-621, 13.1-815.1, 13.1-936.1).

And there may be additional accounting fees. Each year you will need to file separate corporate income tax returns; one for the state and one for the IRS.

You do not need to pay filing fees to the Secretary of State to form a sole proprietorship, and you do not need to file separate income tax returns. You can include your business income as part of your personal income tax return and not go through the cost and hassle of filing a separate corporate return.

Another reason to start a business as a sole proprietorship is the risk of failure. Although every new business owner thinks his venture must surely culminate in riches, research conducted by the Brandow Company shows that only 55% of new businesses get to celebrate their third birthday (see their data at www.brandow.com). You can always form a corporation should your business succeed. If the business does not succeed, then at least you didn't waste time, effort and money to form a corporation.

But What About My Personal Liability?

Many people seek to limit their personal liability by forming a corporation, however, that doesn't always work in the real world. For example, if you wish to rent a store front or office space, an experienced landlord will allow you to lease the space in the corporate name, but he will require you to sign as a guarantor. Should the business fail, he will have the right to sue you, personally, for the full value of the lease. Once you have established a successful business, the landlord may agree to just hold the business liable; and in that case having a corporation instead of a sole proprietorship will limit your personal liability.

Regardless of what form of business ownership you choose, you can be held personally liable for any fraudulent or negligent act that you commit. The way to avoid personal liability for fraudulent acts is not to willfully (deliberately) deceive or cheat anyone.

Most of us are honest folk, but negligence is another matter. We all make mistakes. The way to limit your liability for negligence is to purchase insurance that provides protection for mistakes and accidents. For example, if you open a title insurance business, you can purchase an Errors and Omissions insurance policy to cover a loss caused by a mistake you might make in a title search. If you have any business involving the care of a person (adult or child day care center, nurse practitioner, etc.), it is important to have coverage for an injury to a client due to accident or malpractice.

If you have a business location (a storefront or office) consider purchasing a comprehensive business insurance policy to cover injury to anyone who visits your business, as well as damages to the premises. For example, if you open a flower shop you can get insurance to cover an injury to a customer who slips and falls. The same policy can cover vandalism to your shop, such as a broken plate glass window. You can be compensated for loss should a storm cause the electricity to go out and your shipment of fresh cut flowers wilt for lack of refrigeration.

The purpose of any business insurance policy is to shift the risk of a business loss from your pocket to that of the insurance company.

And the downside is . . .
The problem with insurance is the greater the risk, the greater the cost. We all would like 100% insurance coverage, but few of us can afford the premium. What holds true for life insurance holds true for business insurance. The right amount of insurance coverage for you is the amount that allows you to sleep at night.

A business partnership is much like a marriage. You can both start out with the best of intentions, only to find that you are hopelessly incompatible. The break-up of a business partnership can be just as bitter and hotly contested as the breakup of a marriage. A properly drafted Partnership Agreement is a must — not only to set the terms of a dissolution, but to clearly state what is expected of each partner; i.e., how much each will contribute to the business venture in terms of effort or financing.

The Partnership Agreement should cover what will happen to the partner's share in the event of his incapacity or death. Most Partnership Agreements provide for an appraisal of the business and the buy out of the deceased (or disabled) partner's share. The Partnership Agreement may need to be backed up with financing. For example, you could sign a Partnership Agreement that requires the company to buy out your partnership interest should you become disabled or die. But what good is the Agreement if there is not enough cash in the company to pay for the buy out?

You will have better protection if the Partnership Agreement requires the company to maintain disability and life insurance to pay for the buy out. Many insurance companies offer Key man insurance. The policy is designed to compensate the company for the loss of someone who is essential to the continuation of the business. If sufficient insurance is purchased, the proceeds of the policy can be used to cover any loss suffered by the company and to buy out the share of the company that was owned by the deceased or disabled partner.

COMPANIES THAT LIMIT LIABILITY

The sole proprietorship and the partnership are the earliest type of business organization. Virginia laws governing these types of business organizations have their roots in English Common Law. Common law requires the sole proprietor and each business partner to take full personal responsibility for the debts of the company. As people became ever more litigious (lawyer talk for "sue happy") businessmen sought to limit their liability and prevailed on the legislature to create a form of business ownership to limit that liability.

Legislatures in each state responded to that need by giving businessmen the right to create a company (the corporation) with an identity separate from the owners of the business. By doing business as a corporation, the businessman's liability is limited to the money he invests in the company. A person can sue the corporation for business debts, but not the owners of the corporation.

This does not mean that a corporate owner can use the corporation to do things that are not legal, or morally reprehensible. If he does, he can be held personally liable. He cannot use the corporation as a "veil" to cover his wrongdoing. Courts have ruled that they will "pierce the corporate veil" and hold shareholders, officers and directors personally liable if they use or control a corporation to "... evade a personal obligation, or perpetrate fraud or a crime, to commit an injustice, or to gain an unfair advantage" (*O'Hazza v. Executive Credit Corporation*, 246 Va. 111 (1993); 431 S.E.3d 318).

THE CORPORATION
flexible control — limited liability

Whoever forms a corporation (the *incorporator*) has maximum control over the corporation. He decides how the company will operate by having the company *By-laws* prepared according to his specifications. He can keep full control of the company as the only shareholder, or he can distribute shares and give up as much control as he wishes. Transferring corporate ownership is simple. It is a matter of signing a stock certificate transferring the shares of stock in the company. You can have a Transfer On Death designation to a named beneficiary.

If you own shares of stock in your name only, without a TOD designation, your Personal Representative will transfer the shares according to your Will, or if no Will, according to Virginia's Laws of Descent. But that may not be the best way to go. If Probate is necessary, it may take several months before the shares are transferred to the proper beneficiary, meanwhile, someone needs to continue to operate the business. If you do not leave specific directions for the continuance of the business, the Personal Representative (or the Probate Court) may decide it is best to just sell the company and give the proceeds of the sale to your beneficiaries.

The better route is to have your attorney prepare a Revocable Living Trust and transfer the shares into the Trust. The Trust document can give your Successor Trustee specific instructions about how the business is to be managed or transferred should you become incapacitated or die. Still another important benefit is to avoid the need to Probate what may be your only valuable asset.

THE LIMITED PARTNERSHIP

Just as a sole proprietor can limit his liability by forming a corporation, the partners of a general partnership can limit their liability by converting the partnership to a **Limited Partnership**. As with the corporation, the Limited Partnership is a creation of the legislature and is regulated by Virginia law. The name of the Limited Partnership must identify it as a limited partnership or contain the initials "LP." A Certificate of Limited Partnership must be filed with the State Corporation Commission (VA 50-73.2, 50-73.11).

The structure of a Limited Partnership differs from a general partnership. In a general partnership, each partner has full authority to conduct business on behalf of the partnership. Each partner is personally liable for monies owed by the partnership, regardless of whether that partner actually incurred the debt. The Limited Partnership has *General Partners* and *Limited Partners*. Only a General Partner has authority to conduct partnership business and only a General Partner is liable for company debts. A Limited Partner has no control over the management of the company and has no personal liability for company debts (VA 50-73.24).

But even a General Partner can avoid personal liability by forming a corporation, and then letting the corporation serve as the sole General Partner. An unpaid creditor of the Limited Partnership can sue the corporate General Partner, but not the shareholders of the corporation. Liability can be limited to the amount of money invested in the business venture. None of the owners will have personal liability. Of course, as with the corporation, all parties can be held personally liable for fraudulent or criminal acts performed in their partnership capacity.

The astute reader might be wondering "Why would anyone form a corporation (and pay all of the costs to set up the corporation) and then make the corporation the General Partner of a Limited Partnership (after paying all that money to set up the Partnership)? If limited business liability is the goal, why not just form a corporation?"

Answers to those questions are many and in fact, far removed from the original goal of limiting the business risk of the partners to just the money they invested in the business. The Limited Partnership can be used as a means of transferring a family business to the children with some significant tax benefits. For example, suppose Mom & Pop run a small, highly profitable, rapidly expanding, gourmet chocolate shop. They have two children, both in college. Right now, the business is worth about $500,000, but they figure that by the time they retire, the business could be worth millions. If their children inherit the business at that time, there could be significant Estate Taxes due. Also, because they are making lots of money right now, they are paying very high income taxes.

Both problems can be solved with a Family Limited Partnership. Mom and Pop can be the General Partners of the company and retain total control. They could make each child a Limited Partner by transferring shares of the business worth less than the current Annual Gift Tax Exclusion. That exclusion is currently $11,000, so together Mom and Pop can gift shares of the partnership up to $22,000 per child, per year. By gifting a percentage of the business each year, the parents can eventually transfer all of the business to the children. When the parents die, there will be no Gift or Estate Tax because the children already own the business. Of course there is still the problem of the Capital Gains Tax should the children decide to sell the business.

Regardless of how much of the company they give away, Mom and Pop can keep total control of the company because they are General Partners. When the parents are ready to retire, one or both of the children can take over as General Partner — but if making chocolate is not their thing, the parents can arrange to have a corporation manage the Limited Partnership and the children continue to receive income as limited partners. As for the current income tax problem, the children, as limited partners, are entitled to receive income from the business. Income paid to the children and their parents is generally taxed at a lower rate than the taxes to just Mom and Pop. For example, suppose the company earns $100,000. Mom and Pop will pay a high rate of income tax if they are the only two partners in the company. If the children become partners, then each partner can earn $25,000 and the overall bill for income taxes will be smaller.

Still another important advantage of the Family Limited Partnership over the corporation is creditor protection for the children's partnership interest. For example, suppose one of the children becomes a dentist, gets sued for malpractice, and loses the case. If Mom and Pop had incorporated the business and given the children most of the shares of stock in the company, the creditor could take the shares to satisfy the judgment. The creditor could wind up owning the company! Not so, with a Limited Partnership interest. A judge could order that the income from the Limited Partnership be used to pay the judgment, but he could not order the Partnership share itself to be given to the creditor unless the Limited Partnership Agreement allows for such transfer or unless all other partners agree (VA 50-73.46:1, 50-73.47). Not likely with Mom and Pop as General Partners. They might even decide to use company income to pay themselves salary and not distribute anything to the hapless creditor!

We used an actual business as an example to explain how the Limited Partnership worked. It didn't take Estate Planning attorneys long to figure out that the "family business" could be just income producing items (such as stocks and bonds) that Mom and Pop placed into the Limited Partnership. The family "business" could be just the business of earning income. In other words, the Family Limited Partnership (or even a Family Partnership) could just be a type of an Estate Plan created solely for the purpose of transferring assets to the children to avoid paying Estate Taxes, and to pay less in income taxes.

It didn't take the IRS long to challenge this method of Estate Planning. A series of IRS rulings and court cases followed, with the main issue being whether a bona fide business partnership existed.

There is a common sense rule of evidence that says "If it looks like a duck and walks like a duck, and quacks like a duck, it must be a duck." In 1946 the Supreme Court decided that whether a family partnership is really a business partnership for tax purposes, should be determined on a case by case basis; and that the IRS should use the "walk and quack" test. Only the justices said this in proper legal terms. They said to determine whether a partnership exists depends on ". . .whether the partners really and truly intended to join together for the purpose of carrying on a business and sharing in the profits or losses or both. And their intention in this respect is a question of fact, to be determined from testimony disclosed by their agreement, considered as a whole, and by their conduct in execution of its provisions" (*Commissioner v. Tower*, 327 U.S. 280 (1946)).

THE LIMITED LIABILITY COMPANY

The IRS continues to take a close look at family partnerships, and will challenge any tax break if the family partnership (limited or not) does not meet the basic requirement of being a bona fide business partnership. Perhaps in response to IRS challenges, in the 1990s each of the 50 states, and even the District of Columbia, passed laws enabling residents of their state to form a new business entity called a *Limited Liability Company* ("LLC"). A Virginia LLC is formed by filing Articles of Organization with the State Corporation Commission. This new entity is not required to be a profit making venture. It can transact any lawful business, just the same as a sole proprietorship, partnership, corporation, or any other business organization (VA 13.1-1008, 13.1010, 13.1-1011, 13.1-1012).

The LLC combines the better features of the Limited Partnership and the Corporation. Like the corporation, it can be formed by a single person who sets the rules of the company when he forms the corporation. The set of rules is called an *Operating Agreement*. Members who join the company must agree to act in accordance with the Operating Agreement.

The LLC can be run by a manager (who is not a member of the company) or it can be run by a member or members of the company. As with a corporation, all members have limited liability, regardless of whether that member happens to be managing the company. As with a Limited Partnership, a creditor cannot take possession or control of a share of the company owned by a member. The most the creditor can do is get a court to assign income generated by that share to the creditor (VA 13.1-1002, 13.1-1041).

Now Mom and Pop can form a LLC, give away some or all of the shares of the company during their lifetime, and still keep control of the company, and with no more personal liability than a non-managing member of the Limited Liability Company.

Transfers into the Limited Liability Company can be made so that there are no Estate or Gift Tax consequences. Income can be distributed to the children, or not, as Mom and Pop see fit.

The skeptic is probably thinking "Maximum control, limited liability, easily transferred to my beneficiaries, no Estate Tax. This is too good to be true. There must be a catch somewhere."

And so there is. It's called the Capital Gains Tax. If you transfer property during your lifetime, that property is valued by the IRS as of the date of transfer. If you gift a share of the Limited Liability Company during your lifetime, your beneficiary will take your basis in the property (i.e., the value that you paid for your interest in the Company). If you sell the share to your beneficiary, his basis is the fair market value of the share as of the date of purchase. Either way, once the beneficiary decides to sell the property, there may be a significant Capital Gains Tax due.

An experienced Estate Planning attorney should be able to suggest any number of ways to solve the problem, including purchasing life insurance to pay the tax.

Regardless of what form of business ownership you have, you need to think about what will happen to your business in the event of your incapacity or death. And in particular, how company debts will be paid. If your business is highly leveraged (business talk for "owes lots of money"), you also need to consider how those loans will be paid should you become disabled or die. One solution is to purchase Key man insurance. As explained earlier, Key man insurance is protection for the company against the loss of a valuable employee. The company purchases the policy and the proceeds are paid to the company to compensate it for the loss; but ultimately the policy benefits those who inherit the business.

Taxes are still another concern. Your business may be worth millions on paper, and your Estate Taxes will be based on that value. Your heirs might be forced to sell the company just to pay the taxes, but without your leadership they may get only a fraction of the value of the company.

Even if the federal government decides to eliminate federal Estate Taxes, the state of Virginia, or any other state where you have a business location, may decide to levy an Estate or Inheritance Tax.

And there is still the problem of the Capital Gains Tax. No one in Congress is talking about doing away with the Capital Gains Tax — and that tax could be sizeable. One solution to the problem of an unknown Estate Tax and/or Capital Gains Tax is to purchase life insurance that can be used to pay for any Estate Tax that may be due upon your death and any Capital Gains Tax that may be due when your beneficiary sells the property he inherits.

That may sound like a good simple solution, but you need to think things through before calling your insurance agent. The first question being:

How much insurance should I purchase?
That is a tough question. If you are in good health, who knows what will happen before you die. Will your business increase in value or go bust? Will the federal government really do away with Estate Taxes or will they do nothing and allow the tax to be reinstated in 2011?

The last question is particularly troublesome. Under today's tax law, if you purchase a life insurance policy, or even control the benefits of the policy, all of the proceeds of the policy will be counted as part of your taxable Estate. You may be buying insurance just to pay more in taxes to Uncle Sam.

You don't need a soothsayer or psychic to solve the problem. A financial planner with access to computer generated models can predict your life expectancy, how much your business will be worth when you retire and even the probability that the economy will require Estate taxes to be reinstated!

Suppose your financial planner predicts that Estate Taxes will be reinstated and that your heirs will probably need to pay 1 million dollars. If you purchase a million dollar insurance policy, the value of the policy will be included in your Estate. If there is an Estate Tax of 40% your heirs will net only $600,000 of your million dollar policy, the rest going for Estate taxes on the proceeds of the policy itself.

Your heirs will need to come up with an additional $400,000 to make up for the original million dollars predicted as being necessary to pay your Estate taxes. The solution to this dilemma is the IRREVOCABLE LIFE INSURANCE TRUST.

THE IRREVOCABLE LIFE INSURANCE TRUST

An *Irrevocable Life Insurance Trust* can be designed to provide money to pay any tax that may be due after your death. To be sure that the IRS does not count the proceeds of the Trust as part of your taxable Estate the Trust must meet the following requirements:

    ⇨   The Trust must be irrevocable.

    ⇨   You cannot be Trustee.

The Trust can be set up for the benefit of your child. In such case, the child can be Trustee of the Trust. The child, as Trustee, will purchase an insurance policy on your life. You may need to file a Gift Tax return if you give your child a large sum of money to purchase the policy. It is better to have the child purchase a policy that is paid in quarterly or annual premiums instead of a single lump sum payment. You can give the child an amount each year up to the Annual Gift Tax Exclusion (currently $11,000) to pay for the premium. If you are married, you and your spouse can gift up to $22,000 per year without the need to file a Gift Tax return.

As tax laws change, the child/Trustee can use as much of the gift as is needed to purchase sufficient insurance to cover the taxes. The Trust can be set up to cover Estate Taxes or Capital Gains Taxes, or both. For example, the Trustee can purchase an insurance policy that pays a million dollars upon your death. Those insurance funds can be used to pay your Estate Taxes. Should it happen that no Estate taxes are due, the Trustee can keep the monies invested until the business is sold. The Trust funds can be used to pay any Capital Gains Tax that may be due at that time. If monies are left over once all taxes are paid, they can be distributed to the named beneficiaries of the Trust.

Your attorney can design an Irrevocable Insurance Trust in any number of ways to meet the special needs of you and your family. For example, an Irrevocable Insurance Trust can be set up to solve problems described in the last Chapter. Alan wanted to leave insurance proceeds for his child but was concerned that the cash value of the policy could be taken by his creditors. A properly drafted Irrevocable Insurance Trust can solve such problem, because the Trust, and not Alan, is the owner of the policy.

Of course, it costs significant money to set up and maintain an Irrevocable Insurance Trust. Those who do not have concerns about creditors may wonder whether it's necessary to go through all that cost and bother if there will be no more Estate Taxes in the future. After all a simple life insurance policy can cover any Capital Gains Tax that may be due. But, as explained, the tax law as passed in 2001 reinstates the Estate Tax in 2011. If lawmakers take no further action, the Estate of anyone who dies on January 1, 2011, and thereafter is subject to an Estate Tax for an Estate over one million dollars.

Someone with an active imagination could envision the following scenario:

It is New Year's eve, 2010. A 97 year old lies sleeping, at his home, surrounded by his four grandchildren who are his sole heirs.

"He looks so peaceful."

"Yes. Surprising, considering that he has terminal cancer, failing kidneys and heart. His doctor says he can't last more than a few days. The doctor left a supply of morphine so that we can keep Gramps comfortable over the New Year's holiday. The doctor gave him a shot just before he left."

"The doctor said not to give Gramps another shot unless he was in pain. His heart is in such a weakened condition, he could easily overdose on morphine."

"Yes, of course."

"Too bad he didn't get a chance to do some Estate Planning before he had that stroke last year. "

"I thought his attorney took care of all that."

"His attorney suggested he set up an Irrevocable Insurance Trust to pay for any Estate Tax, but Gramps felt sure that Congress would pass a law that would permanently repeal the Estate Tax."

"I can't imagine Gramps coming to that conclusion. The economy is down and the government needs to raise taxes. It is easier for legislators to leave the law as written back in 2001, than take some affirmative action."

"Gramps was always a sharp business man, but in his later years his mind wasn't as clear as when he earned his five million dollars."

"Is that what we are going to inherit?"

"Not unless he dies before midnight. After midnight the Estate Tax is reinstated, and at a rate of 45%. Between state and federal taxes, we'll be lucky to come away with half a mill each."

"Gramps moved. I think he may be in pain."

"Yes, he does look uncomfortable."

"It isn't right to let him suffer like this."

"Yes, of course."

Continuing To Care 7

There are any number of reasons that people give for wanting to continue on with their lives. For the lucky ones, their main reason for living is that they are having a great time and don't want it to end. For many, it is more a sense of responsibility. During child rearing years the concern of the parent is what will happen to the child should the parent suddenly die. Once a child is grown, the roles often reverse, and it is the child worrying about what will happen to his parent if the child were not present to see to the care of the aging parent. Even pet lovers worry about what will happen to their pet should the owner no longer be around.

There is little that can be done to prepare those who depend on you for the loss of your companionship and emotional support; but there are many things you can do to provide financial support for those who rely on you. Even people of modest means can make financial provision so their loved ones will have an easy transition from being dependent to becoming self sufficient.

This chapter explains the many simple, and relatively inexpensive, things you can do to provide care for your loved ones should you not be present to do so yourself.

CARING FOR THE MINOR CHILD

It doesn't happen very often, but both parents could die or become incapacitated before their child reaches adulthood. Most parents don't want to think about, much less prepare for such a happening. But in this age of postponing parenthood, many parents are in their fifties and sixties and still raising children. The probability of a life threatening illness increases with age, so parents need to understand the importance of planning ahead.

Parents with dangerous occupations also need to provide for the care of their minor child in the event of the disability or death of both parents. It is surprising to think of how many of us are employed in dangerous occupations. Construction workers, military personnel, firemen, state and federal law enforcement agents, and in this day and age, even postal workers face hazards on a daily basis.

Regardless of the parent's age or occupation, planning for the care of a minor child should be part of every parent's Estate Plan, not only because it is the responsible thing to do, but also because it is relatively simple and inexpensive to do.

A child must be cared for in two ways, the **person** of the child and the **property** of the child. To care for the person of the child, someone must be in charge of the child's everyday living, not only food and shelter but to provide social, ethical and religious training. Someone must have legal authority to make medical decisions and see to the child's education. To care for the child's property, someone must be responsible to see that monies left to the child are used for the care of the child and that anything left over is preserved until the child becomes an adult.

If both parents are unable to care for the person of a minor, the Probate Court will appoint someone to serve as the Guardian until the child's 18th birthday. The Court may give the Guardian authority to care for the child's property as well, but if the child's assets are significant the Court may decide to appoint a **Conservator** to manage the property. The Conservator will be responsible to see that sufficient monies are used for the care of the child and that anything left over is preserved until the child is an adult (VA 37.1-134.8).

USING A WILL TO APPOINT A GUARDIAN

As explained in Chapter 4, you have the right to name some-one in your Will to serve as your child's Guardian, in the event that the other parent is deceased or incapacitated. You can appoint someone to serve as the Guardian of the child's person, and another to serve as the Guardian of the child's property, or you can name someone to serve in both capacities (person and property).

If you leave property for the child in your Will, you can name anyone you wish to serve as the Guardian of that property. The person you name as Guardian of gifts that you leave to your child has the right to serve in that capacity regardless of whether there is a surviving parent (VA 31-2).

In the event the other parent is incapacitated or does not survive you, whoever you appoint in your Will to serve as Guardian can take over upon your death; but that person is not the legal Guardian until a Judge of a Circuit Court makes it official. It is important that the person you choose to serve as Guardian be ready and willing to serve, be-cause if he does not apply within six months of your death, the Court can appoint someone else for the job (VA 31-3, 31-14).

THE BEST CHOICE OF GUARDIAN

It is a good idea for both parents to name the same person to serve as Guardian. If the child's parents appoint different people for the job and then die simultaneously, it will be up to the Judge to decide who is best suited to be Guardian. If they do not die simultaneously, then the Court will give top priority to the person named in the Will of the last parent to die.

Many parents never get around to appointing a Guardian because they cannot come to an agreement as to the best choice of Guardian. "I think my mother should be Guardian. After all she raised me, and I turned out fine" can signal the opening salvo of a lengthy, and often unresolved battle. Not being able to agree on a choice of Guardian should not discourage you from appointing the person of your choice either as part of your Will or in a separate writing. The thing to keep in mind is that the Guardian of your choice will take over only if the other parent is deceased or incapacitated. Even if you both die simultaneously, and you each name someone different to serve as Guardian, your choice of Guardian will at least be brought to the attention of the Court.

If neither parent has expressed his choice of Guardian, the appointment will be up to the Court. If the child is at least 14, the Judge will appoint the child's choice of Guardian, provided that person is qualified and willing to be Guardian (VA 31-5).

One problem with using a Will to appoint someone to be your child's Guardian, is that for the appointment to be effective, the Will must be admitted to Probate; i.e., the Court must determine that the Will is valid; and the person you chose as Guardian needs to file a petition to be appointed as the child's Guardian.

It might take several weeks before that person has the legal authority to care for the child. A better solution is to appoint someone as a STANDBY GUARDIAN who can immediately assume responsibility for the care of the minor child, should the need arise.

THE STANDBY GUARDIAN

It may happen that a parent who has sole custody of a child becomes seriously ill and in jeopardy of not being able to care for the child. Under such circumstance the parent can appoint a *Standby Guardian* to care for the child in the event of the parent's incapacity or death. The parent can do so by signing a DESIGNATION OF STANDBY GUARDIAN. The designation must be prepared and signed as described in Virginia statute 16.1-352.

Even a healthy parent should consider signing a DESIGNATION OF STANDBY GUARDIAN to appoint a Standby Guardian for his/her minor child. It is important to do so should the parent with sole custody of the child be a member of the armed forces or work in any dangerous line of work.

You can prepare the Designation of Standby Guardian yourself, but it is best to have an attorney assist you. If you cannot afford an attorney, there are any number of Legal Services who can help you for little or no charge. See page xii for information about how to locate your nearest Legal Service office.

The Standby Guardian can take over as soon as he is notified that the parent is unable to care for the child; however within thirty (30) days, the Standby Guardian must petition (ask) the Court in the county of the child's residence for Court's approval to serve as the minor's Standby Guardian (VA 16.1-352 (D)).

If the parent dies, the Standby Guardian must, within 90 days, petition the Court to appoint a legal Guardian for the child (VA 16.1-353).

The DESIGNATION OF STANDBY GUARDIAN is not limited to a minor child. The parent of a mentally retarded or developmentally disabled person can use the Designation to appoint someone to take over should the parent become incapacitated or die. If the child is over 18, and not profoundly handicapped, the child may object to having a Guardian. In such case, there will need to be a Court hearing to determine whether the adult child is in need of a guardian of the person or property, or both. It may take considerable time to collect sufficient evidence of the need (or lack of it) for the Court to rule.

The solution to the problem is to have the parent petition the Court to legally appoint a Standby Guardian, and an alternate Standby Guardian to serve in the event that the appointed Standby Guardian cannot serve as guardian. The Court will hold a hearing on the matter. Any issue of the child's need for a Guardian can be settled at that hearing.

Once the Standby Guardian is appointed by the Court, should the parent become disabled or die, the Standby Guardian can immediately take over. The Court appointed Standby Guardian must still apply to the Court to be appointed as the legal guardian (VA 15.1-351).

As any parent is well aware, it is expensive to raise a child. The person you consider to be the best choice to serve as Guardian might not be able to do so unless you leave sufficient monies to pay for the care of the child. If you have limited finances, consider purchasing a term life insurance policy on your life and/or on the life of the other parent of the child. If you can only afford one policy, insure the life of the parent who contributes most to the support of the child.

Term insurance policies are relatively inexpensive if you limit the term to just that period of time until your child becomes an adult. Some companies offer a combination of term life and disability insurance, in the event that the bread-winner becomes disabled and unable to work. As with any other purchase, it is important to comparison shop to obtain the best price for the coverage.

If you are married, you may want to name your spouse as the beneficiary of the term insurance policy with your child as an alternate beneficiary. Married or single, you can name your child as the primary beneficiary of the policy. Under Virginia law, the insurance company may give amounts up to $10,000 to the parent or Guardian of the child. The insurance company is required to seek Court permission before transferring funds that exceed that amount. If the sum to be transferred is substantial, the Court will probably require a Guardian or a Conservator to be appointed to protect the funds until the child reaches 18 (VA 8.01-606).

The insurance company is not required to transfer funds under $10,000. They may decide to ask for Court authority to make any transfer where a minor is involved.

We discussed the ways parents can control who is appointed to serve as the Guardian of their minor child should both parents be incapacitated or deceased. Guardianship is a necessity in such cases. But if at least one of the parents is able to care for the person of the child, it may be wise to avoid the need for the Court to appoint a Guardian of the property. If you leave the child a significant amount of money the Court will appoint a Guardian of that property. Even if the surviving parent is appointed to serve as Guardian, the amount you leave to the child will be reduced by the cost of establishing and maintaining the guardianship.

An attorney must be employed to establish the guardianship. Once appointed, the Guardian has many duties. He must prepare an inventory and file an annual accounting with the Court. The Guardian may need to employ an accountant to assist with the preparation of the inventory and the annual accounting. Depending on the size of the Estate, the Guardian of the property may need to employ a financial advisor to manage the property. All these fees are proper charges to the child's guardianship property (VA 26-12, 26-17.4, 26-30).

Monies left for the care of the child may be significantly reduced by the cost of caring for the property. This can be avoided by leaving property to the child in such a manner, that will make it unnecessary for the Court to appoint a Guardian of the property of the child. One way to do so is to include a Trust for the child as part of your Will. Another is to set up a Revocable Living Trust that includes provisions for the care of the child. If you have limited finances, a good alternative is to appoint someone to serve as Custodian of the gift under the VIRGINIA UNIFORM TRANSFERS TO MINORS ACT.

THE UNIFORM TRANSFERS TO MINORS ACT

The **Virginia Uniform Transfers to Minors Act** is designed to protect gifts made to a minor by appointing someone to be the **Custodian** of a gift until the child is an adult. For example, you can make a minor child the beneficiary of your life insurance policy, and name a trusted relative or friend or even a financial institution to be the Custodian of the gift. Should you die while the child is a minor, the insurance company will give the proceeds of the policy to the person you named as Custodian to hold until the child is an adult.

You can make a gift to a minor in your Will. You can appoint your Personal Representative (or anyone else) as Custodian of the gift. For example:

I give the sum of $20,000 to _____(name)
as custodian for _____ (name of minor)
under the Virginia Uniform Transfers to Minors Act.

THE LIFETIME GIFT

You can even use the Virginia Uniform Transfers to Minors Law to make a gift during your lifetime of some item such as shares in a corporation or a limited partnership interest. You can nominate yourself as Custodian of the gift, or you can name another person to serve as Custodian. Once the lifetime gift is made it becomes irrevocable, so this method is not appropriate unless you are sure that you want the child to have the gift once he/she is an adult (VA 31-39, 31-41).

In general, the Custodian must distribute the gift when the child reaches 18; however, if you make a lifetime gift, or a gift as part of your Will, you can direct the Custodian to distribute the gift when the child reaches 21 (VA 31-45).

THE CUSTODIAN'S DUTIES

Under Virginia law, while the Custodian is in possession of the gift, he can use as much of the gift as he thinks advisable for the benefit of the child. He can pay monies directly to the child, or use the funds for the child's benefit. In making the distribution he is not obliged to take into account that someone else has a duty to support the child — even if the Custodian is the child's parent and it is his own responsibility to support the child (VA 31-50).

The Custodian can do the opposite and distribute nothing. He can refuse to use any of the monies for the child and just keep the funds invested until the funds are distributed when the child is an adult. In such case, the child's parent or Guardian (or even the child once he is 14) can ask a Court to order that the monies be used for the care of the child. The Judge will determine what is in the child's best interest and then rule on the matter.

Hopefully, the Custodian will give a regular accounting to the child's parent or guardian. If not, any member of the child's family, or the child once he/she reaches 14, can ask the Court to order a full accounting of the custodial property (VA 31-55).

As with any type of Estate Plan, you need to examine all aspects of the transfer to see if there is anything that may be objectionable to you.

THE CUSTODIAN'S FEE

The law requires the Custodian to invest and manage the property in a responsible, prudent manner. The Custodian is entitled to be paid for his effort. If the gift is sizeable, his fee can be sizeable. Before appointing a person or a financial institution as Custodian, it is best to come to a written agreement about how the property will be managed and the charge for doing so (VA 31-51).

NO GROUP GIFT

You cannot make a gift to more than one child under the Uniform Transfers To Minors Act. For example, you cannot make a single gift of real property to two or more minor children under the Uniform Transfers To Minors Act. If you wanted to make such a gift, you would need do so by another method, such as creating a Trust for the children (VA 31-46).

THE COST OF PROBATE

As discussed, you can include a gift to a minor in your Will by naming a Custodian for the gift. As with any gift made under a Will, a Probate procedure will be necessary to distribute the gift to the Custodian. This may not be the best way to go, if you are trying to avoid Probate. If your gift is significant, the better route is to set up a Revocable Living Trust. You can manage the Trust while you are able. Should you become incapacitated or die before the child is grown your Successor Trustee will take over. Unlike the Uniform Gift to Minors, you can direct the Trustee to give the gift to the child at any age you think proper.

Which brings us to another problem, namely, that there is no flexibility as to the final distribution of a gift made under the Uniform Transfers to Minors Act.

MANDATORY DISTRIBUTION

A Custodian appointed under the Uniform Transfers To Minors Act must distribute the gift by the child's 18th birthday (21st if your Will or lifetime gift so directs) (VA 31-56). The gift must be made regardless of whether the child has sufficient maturity to handle the money in a responsible manner. A sizeable gift to an immature beneficiary is not the best Estate Plan.

PROVIDING FOR THE STEPCHILD

Perhaps the reason that the story of Cinderella has such universal appeal is that many stepchildren, at one point or another, feel left out. The law seems to reinforce that perception. Unless a married person makes provision otherwise, a spouse has priority over the child in health matters both before and after death. If a married person is too ill to make medical decisions, the doctors will turn to the spouse for directions. Should a married person die, the decedent's spouse and not the child, has the authority to agree to an autopsy or anatomical gift (VA 32.1-290.1, 54.1-2825, 54.1-2973).

If a married couple hold all of their property jointly, that property will go to the surviving spouse and not to the child of the deceased parent. This might not be a problem if the surviving spouse is the natural parent of the child. It could be a major problem if the natural parent dies first. The stepchild of the surviving parent may be left with nothing.

In such situations, the stepparent comes across as villain, but it is the parent, and not the stepparent, who decides whether the child will inherit property belonging to the natural parent. Too often the stepchild is left out by default, i.e., the natural parent doesn't give the matter any thought, or perhaps the natural parent is confident that the stepparent will do "what's right."

That was the case with Walter. He always wanted to be a father, so he was pleased when Todd was born just before the first anniversary of Walter's marriage to Nancy. Twin girls were born just 15 months later. Unfortunately the twins' birth was premature, causing them to have medical and developmental problems. Nancy had her hands full just caring for the three children, so it was up to Walter to support the family.

Walter was up to the job. He was both conscientious and ambitious. He started his own interior decorating business, complete with a retail sales storefront to sell fabrics, and an upholstery shop in the rear of the store. With hard work and long hours, he was able to make a comfortable living. But the strain of raising a family and running a business took its toll, both on him and the marriage. At 40, he felt like an old man.

All that changed when he hired Annie to manage the retail part of his business. Her energy and sunny disposition were just what the business (and Walter) needed.

Walter's divorce from Nancy was amicable. Walter was a loving father who took his responsibilities seriously. He was generous when it came to supporting the children. Walter had only finished high school, and he wanted more for his son. He encouraged Todd to do well in school so that he could go on to college, and maybe become a doctor or lawyer. The twins had developmental problems; but Walter encouraged them to reach their maximum potential. It was his goal to help them become self sufficient.

Annie got along very well with her stepchildren. She had no trouble with Walter's desire to support the children and give them a good start in life. Even though they held all of their money in a joint account, she never questioned any expense made on behalf of the children.

Walter never gave much thought to an Estate Plan. After all, he was healthy, and in the prime of his earning capacity. He often said that he was fortunate to have married two wonderful women. If he had a dark thought, it soon passed, rationalizing that if something happened to him, Annie would take care of the children.

But she didn't.

Walter died in one of those freak accidents. He was trimming the branches from his tree with an electric saw and accidentally touched an overhead wire. All he owned was tied up in the business that he held jointly with Annie. Annie felt that she was a major factor in the success of that business. Why should she share any of her hard earned money with Nancy? As for the children, it was Nancy's job to raise them. After all they were Nancy's children, and not Annie's children. If it was a struggle to support the children, then that was Nancy's problem!

A better argument (but one she didn't raise) was that Walter really wanted Annie to inherit everything. If he wanted to provide for his children, he could have done so in any number of different ways, beginning with his marriage to Annie:

✍ He could have insisted on a prenuptial agreement that would have provided for certain funds to be kept separate for the benefit of his children.

✍ He could have signed a partnership agreement with Annie that would have given his share of the business to his children, in the event of his death.

✍ If he didn't want to negotiate with Annie about a prenuptial agreement or a partnership agreement, he could have had his attorney prepare a Trust that would have cared for the children until they were old enough to be on their own.

✍ If nothing else, he could have purchased a life insurance policy with the children as beneficiaries of the policy.

THE SECOND MARRIAGE TRUST

Walter's situation is not unique. Second marriages are commonplace in America. Many who are widowed or divorced, remarry. If children are involved, the parent may have divided loyalties. The parent may want to provide income to the child until the child completes his education, and then leave whatever is left of his Estate to his surviving spouse. More often it is the other way around. The parent wants to be sure that the surviving spouse has sufficient income to support his/her current life-style, but once the surviving spouse dies, the parent wants all that remains to go to his children. A properly drafted Trust can provide for the care of a spouse and child in whatever way the Grantor of the Trust thinks best.

That was the case with an elderly widower who married a pretty girl less than half his age. Their prenuptial agreement made it clear that all his property would go to his son from his first marriage. Surprisingly, the marriage turned out well. So well that the couple had two daughters. The husband decided to divide his Estate equally among his three children and to provide for the care of his wife until the youngest child was grown.

His attorney suggested a Trust. "You can be Trustee during your lifetime. Once you die, your Successor Trustee can immediately distribute one-third of the Trust to your son who is now 55. No sense to keep him waiting. The rest of your money can remain in your Trust. Income from the Trust can be used to support your wife and children until the youngest is 25. Then, whatever remains in the Trust can be distributed equally to your daughters."

"Good idea" said the elderly gentlemen, with a smile "Just make sure it is revocable during my lifetime. Who knows what adventures I might be up to in the future?"

It isn't just stepchildren who can be left out if no provision is made. Even children from a long-standing marriage can be cut off against the wishes of a parent. A parent may assume that all of their children will be treated equally when both parents are gone, but if all their property is held jointly, the last parent to die is the one who gets to decide "who gets what." Too often, the wishes of the deceased parent are ignored, for example:

THE STRAINED RELATIONSHIP A child may have a close relationship with one parent, and a strained, but tolerable, relationship with the other. Peace in the family is achieved because the parent who is close to the child acts as a buffer. Should the buffer parent die first, the relationship between the surviving parent and the child may fall apart altogether and the child's inheritance be cut off.

THE PARENT WITH DIMINISHED CAPACITY The more common scenario, is that the surviving parent becomes increasingly dependent on one child — either for emotional support, or for physical assistance as the parent ages. The other children may live at a distance, or perhaps they are too involved with their own family to assist. The supporting child may end up with most, if not all, of what was intended for all of the children.

These problems can be avoided by having your attorney prepare a Family Trust. The family assets are placed in the Trust with the parents as co-Trustees. The beneficiaries of the Trust cannot be changed unless both parents agree to the change. Once one parent dies, the Trust becomes irrevocable. The Trust income goes to the surviving parent and once that parent dies, whatever remains in the Trust is distributed in the manner as was agreed by both parents.

If you are the caregiver of someone who is incapacitated, then in addition to preparing your own Estate plan, you need to be concerned about who will care for the incapacitated person should something happen to you. Someone will need to make medical decisions for the incapacitated person and see to it that he/she is properly housed and fed. We discussed the appointment of a Standby Guardian to care for a developmentally disabled child. The same strategy can be used to care for an adult who is incapacitated because of age, or disease.

An aged spouse, caring for his incapacitated spouse, may be concerned about who will care for his ill spouse should he die first. Often a family member will agree to take responsibility for the care of an incapacitated person. But perhaps no one wants the job. If there are large sums of money involved it may be the opposite case, too many people may want to be in control. One family member may want the incapacitated spouse to remain at home with the assistance of a home health care worker. Another may think the best place is an assisted living facility with 24 hour care. The caregiver spouse may be concerned that a tug-of-war will erupt over who should serve as Guardian once he dies.

To avoid the problem, the attorney may suggest that a Court approved Standby Guardian be appointed. He may also suggest that a Trust be established to care for the incapacitated person. The only problem with establishing a Trust is the possible loss of government benefits. To avoid that problem the attorney can draft a **SPECIAL NEEDS TRUST.**

A TRUST FOR THE DISABLED

Government assistance is available to provide medical and custodial care for those who are disabled and without the means to care for themselves. Both state and federal government provide such assistance with programs such as Social Security disability benefits and Medicaid. The family often supplements the government program by providing for the incapacitated person's *special needs* or *supplemental needs* such as hobbies, special education, outings to a movie or a sports event — things that give the incapacitated person some quality of life. This is not a problem while family members are alive and able to provide for the incapacitated person. The worry is how to continue that care should the provider die.

To be eligible for government assistance programs the incapacitated person must essentially be without funds. Family members fear that leaving money to the incapacitated person in a Will or Trust will disqualify him from receiving government assistance. Parents of a disabled child may decide to solve the problem by leaving the money to a sibling or other family member with verbal instructions to take care of the child once the parent is deceased.

The problem with that approach is that once the funds are left to the family member, they become his property. Property belonging to the family member is available to his creditors. The funds could be lost in a divorce, or the family member could die and the funds inherited by someone who is not willing to care for the disabled child.

A better solution is to have an experienced Elder Law attorney set up a **Supplemental Needs Trust.** The Trust can be funded by the parent during his lifetime, or after his death by making the Trust the beneficiary of his Will or Trust. It can also be funded by a life insurance policy on the life of the parent. The parent can purchase the policy and name the Supplemental Needs Trust as the beneficiary of the insurance funds.

The Trustee of the Supplemental Needs Trust can use the monies in the Trust to provide for the child's supplemental or special needs during his lifetime. The Trust Agreement can provide that upon the death of the incapacitated person, whatever remains in the Trust be distributed to whoever the parent names as the remainder beneficiary of the Trust.

 NOT RECOMMENDED FOR DISABLED SPOUSE

The Trust we have just described is appropriate for a disabled child, who has no funds of his own. The Trust is funded with monies owned by a parent and not the child. This Trust may not be the way to go if the disabled person is married and the Trust is funded by monies owned by the well spouse. When determining eligibility, the government considers monies owned by both the husband and wife. If a Trust is set up using money owned by either of them, the government will consider the Trust funds to be available to pay for the care of the disabled spouse (42 U.S.C.1382c(a)(3), 1396p(d)(4)(A)).

In Chapter 10 we will discuss how a married couple can arrange their finances to provide for their maintenance without jeopardizing the right of the incapacitated person to qualify for medical assistance.

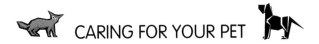 CARING FOR YOUR PET

A woman died at peace,
leaving her fortune
and care of her cat to her niece.
Alas, the fortune and the cat
disappeared soon after that.

You could leave money to someone with the understanding that the person will take care of your pet, but the moral of the above limerick, is that just leaving money will not guarantee care for your pet. The better route is to have your attorney prepare a Will that includes specific instructions and funds to provide for the care of your pet during its lifetime. Those with a Trust can include a similar provision as part of the Trust. The provision for your pet should include directions saying how the remaining funds are to be distributed after the death of the pet.

A TRUST TO CARE FOR YOUR PET

If you are financially able and have several pets, you may want to set up a special Trust for the care of your pets. The person you name as Trustee will be charged with the duty to use Trust funds to pay for the care of those animals who survive you.

You also need to name a residuary beneficiary (a person or perhaps a charitable organization) to receive whatever remains in the Trust once all of the animals are deceased. Animal support groups, such as the Humane Society, have people who will care for the pet of a deceased owner. You might consider appointing such group as the remainder beneficiary of the Trust in exchange for the lifetime care of your pet(s).

If you don't have the resources to set up a Trust to care for your pet, you can still ask a fellow pet lover to care for the animal. If no one among your circle of family and friends is able to do so, then ask your pet's veterinarian to consider starting an "Orphaned Pet Service" to assist in finding new homes for pets who lose their owners. It is good public relations and a potential source of income. If this is agreeable to the Veterinarian, you can make arrangements in your Will to pay the Vet to care for the pet until a suitable family can be found. This is a more humane approach than the, all too common practice, of putting a pet "to sleep" rather than have the pet suffer the loss of its master. And in at least one case, that reasoning backfired.

Eleanor always had a pet in the house. After her husband died, her two poodles were her constant companions. When Eleanor became ill with cancer, she worried about what would happen to her "buddies" without her to care for them. She finally decided it best to have her family put them to sleep when she died.

Eleanor endured surgery, chemotherapy, radiation therapy, and even some holistic remedies, but she continued to go downhill. Eleanor's family came in to visit her at the hospital to say their last good-byes. She was so ill, she didn't even recognize them. No one thought she could last the day. Because the family was from out of state, and time short, they decided to put the pets to sleep so they need only take care of the funeral arrangements when she died.

To everyone's surprise, Eleanor rallied. She lived two more long, lonely years.

She often said she wished they had put her to sleep instead of her buddies.

THE CHARITABLE TRUST

We explained how a Trust can be set up to care for a pet and whatever is left over (the remainder) given to a charitable organization. There are other kinds of charitable trusts that can be set up to benefit the giver as well as the receiver. For example, suppose you own stock which has appreciated substantially over the years, but pays few dividends. This hasn't been a problem in the past because you earned a good income. But now you wish to retire, and will need additional income. You would like to cash in the stock and invest the funds in something that can supplement your retirement income, but your accountant says that a significant portion of the value of the stock will go to Uncle Sam as payment for the Capital Gains Tax.

By now you know that a clever Estate Planning attorney will have any number of ways to solve the problem. The dialogue with your attorney might go something like this:

ATTORNEY: "Do you have a favorite charity?"

"Yes, why do you ask?"

ATTORNEY: "You can set up a Charitable Remainder Trust and donate the stock to that charity by depositing the stock in the Trust. Charities don't pay taxes, so the stock can be sold and the proceeds invested in property that produces a good income. In return for the donation, you can receive an income for the next 20 years or you can receive a monthly Annuity based on your life expectancy."

"What's in it for the charity?"

ATTORNEY: "The charity gets whatever is left after paying you the Annuity."

"Yes, but suppose I die next year, and my wife is left without the securities and no income."

ATTORNEY: "No problem. If you decide on a 20 year Annuity, you can name your wife or any other beneficiary to receive the balance of the Annuity. If you wish, you can have an Annuity based on your life expectancy and that of your spouse. If you predecease your spouse, then the income continues until she dies."

"It seems to me that if the Annuity is based on my life expectancy AND my wife's life expectancy, there won't be much left for the charity."

ATTORNEY: "How much is left for the charity depends on the value of the gift and the cost of the Annuity. The cost of the Annuity depends on the combined life expectancy of you and your wife. I think the best way to understand this plan is for you to look at actual numbers. There are any number of ways to set up a Charitable Remainder Trust. I can explain each option to you. For each option, I will give you the cost of setting up the program; the amount of money you will get, and how much money will actually go to your favorite charity. Of course it must be an IRS approved charity. Once you see the numbers you can make an informed decision as to whether you want to sell the stock and pay the Capital Gains Tax, or set up a Charitable Trust and receive an income."

"Good idea."

THE FUTURE OF ESTATE PLANNING

Up till now Estate Planning for the wealthy was all about the Estate Tax. Estate Planning attorneys would spend their time dreaming up different ways to reduce Estate taxes for their wealthy clients. The IRS would spend their time examining and challenging any Estate plan that appeared too innovative. It seems likely that by 2010 the Estate Tax will be a memory. Is the game over?

Hardly. As explained in Chapter 3, instead of paying an Estate Tax, the child who inherits property that has appreciated more than 1.3 million dollars will pay a substantial Capital Gains Tax when he sells the property. In a way, that makes sense. A major criticism of the Estate Tax was that the tax had to be paid within 9 months of the date of death. That created a hardship for those inheriting a small business with a high assessed value but with no cash to pay taxes on that value.

Critics of the Estate Tax often cited the example of the cash poor farm located on valuable land. Once the owner of the farm died, the family would be forced to sell the farm just to pay Estate Taxes. By substituting the Capital Gains tax for the Estate Tax, that problem is eliminated. No Capital Gains Tax need be paid until the beneficiary decides to sell the property. Theoretically, the family farm can now be inherited generation to generation with no tax consequence.

But there are few family farms in today's economy. Future heirs are more likely to inherit highly appreciated real property or securities that they will eventually want to sell. And when they do, they may need to pay a significant Capital Gains Tax.

The new game for Estate Planning attorneys will be to devise an Estate Plan that will reduce the Capital Gains Tax. The IRS will, no doubt, enjoy challenging those plans.

One tried (and legal) method of reducing the Capital Gains Tax is the Charitable Remainder Trust as was just discussed. It doesn't take a crystal ball to see that this could well be the basis of future Estate Plans, so we will take a few more pages to describe the pros and cons of the Trust.

THE CHARITABLE REMAINDER ANNUITY TRUST

A ***Charitable Remainder Annuity Trust*** is a Trust that is established according to the Internal Revenue Code (IRC 664). Charities do not pay taxes, so property donated to the Trust can be sold by the Trustee free of the Capital Gains Tax. Money from the sale is invested so that it provides an income (an *Annuity*) to the beneficiary (the *Annuitant*) for a fixed period of time, say 20 years, or for the Annuitant's lifetime as computed by actuarial tables (i.e., life expectancy tables). The charity receives whatever is left (the *remainder*) after payment of the Annuity. How much income the donor will receive and how much the charity will receive, is agreed upon at the time the Trust is set up.

The Trust can be set up in any number of ways depending on the goal of the ***donor*** (the person making the gift). In the example just given, the goal of the donor was to convert non-income producing property to income producing property without paying a high Capital Gains Tax. A wealthy donor may be more concerned about his child paying a high Capital Gains Tax should the child inherit highly appreciated property.

For example, suppose you bought acreage in West Virginia that appreciated significantly over the years and is now worth 1 million dollars. You have been putting off selling the property because of the Capital Gains Tax. But it has been a burden to you. It produces no income and because the property continues to appreciate, each year you are paying more and more in property taxes. You did not mind the sacrifice because you figured that your son would inherit the property at a step-up in basis. But now with the new tax law, by the time you die, the property may be worth 2 million dollars. He is only allowed a 1.3 million dollar step up in basis, so your son may need to pay a significant Capital Gains Tax when he sells the property.

Setting up a Charitable Remainder Annuity Trust solves the problem of the Capital Gains Tax. The land is transferred to the Charitable Trust. Charities pay no tax, so the Trustee can sell the land and the full market value of the property will be available for investment.

The Trust could be set up with you receiving an income for life, and your son receiving the Annuity after your death. The only problem with this arrangement is that your son is significantly younger than you are. There may not be much left to benefit the charity if they must wait for both of you to die. The solution is to have the Annuity based on your life only and then use part of the income that you receive to purchase a 2 million dollar insurance policy on your life with your son as beneficiary. The 2 million dollars is the estimated value of the land that your son would have inherited at your death. But with this arrangement he will inherit the insurance proceeds free of any Capital Gains Tax.

The astute reader (and probably one with an accounting background) will say "Aha, you may have avoided the Capital Gains Tax, but the Estate Tax Exclusion value does not increase to 2 million dollars until the year 2006. The 2 million dollar life insurance policy counts as part of your taxable Estate, so if you die before 2006, your son will pay an Estate Tax! "

And of course our clever imaginary attorney has a solution in the form of an Irrevocable Insurance Trust. You can set up an Irrevocable Trust so that the Trust owns the insurance policy and not you. The insurance policy is not included in your taxable Estate, so your son pays no Estate Tax. See the end of Chapter 6 for an explanation of how the Irrevocable Insurance Trust works.

As with any Estate Plan you need to consider the downside, and the Charitable Remainder Annuity Trust is no exception.

⊠   ATTORNEY FEES
It may cost significant attorney fees to set up the Trust. Some charities may offer to have their attorney prepare the Trust at no cost to you, or perhaps they offer a "standard" Trust document that their attorney prepared. But, using their Trust document represents a conflict of interest. Their Trust was prepared by an attorney for the greatest benefit to his client (that's the charity, not you). It is important that you employ your own attorney to represent you. He knows the extent of your Estate and he understands what you wish to accomplish.

☒   THE COMPLEXITY OF THE PLAN

A Charitable Remainder Annuity Trust is a sophisticated Estate Plan designed to benefit the well-to-do donor and an IRS approved charity. There are any number of ways to set up the plan. It is important to have an attorney who will take the time to explore different plans until you determine the best plan for you.

☒   THE TRUST IS IRREVOCABLE

Once established, the Trust is not revocable, so it is important that you understand all of the aspects of the Trust. In particular, you need to know how much it will cost in attorney's fees to set up the Trust; and how much income you will receive, and over what period of time. The income you receive as an Annuitant is taxable to you. You need to consider that while taxes change over the years, the terms of the Trust cannot be changed. It is important that your attorney, accountant or financial planner give you some idea of what you might expect in terms of future income tax payments.

Although future income tax payments may be a question mark, the power of the Charitable Remainder Trust is the tax benefit to the donor at the time the Trust is set up.

☑   NO CAPITAL GAINS TAX

Had you sold the property and invested the money yourself, you would have paid a Capital Gains Tax and that tax could have been substantial, depending on the tax rate in effect at the time of the transfer. By gifting the property the full value of the land can be used to produce investment income.

☑   NO PROPERTY TAX

Once your property is transferred into the Trust, you will no longer need to pay annual property taxes.

☑ NO GIFT TAX

The property you transfer into the Trust is a gift to a charity and as such is not included in the sum total of taxable gifts that you give during your lifetime.

☑ INCOME TAX DEDUCTION

Because you are making a charitable donation, you should be able to take a charitable deduction on your income tax in the year of the donation.

There are other "perks" in addition to the tax benefits:

☑ NO PROBATE EXPENSE

It might take an expensive and time consuming Probate procedure to transfer the property to a beneficiary upon your death. By transferring the property to the Trust during your lifetime, you avoid the need for a Probate procedure to transfer the property after your death.

☑ GIVE WHEN NEEDED INSTEAD OF LATER

A Charitable Remainder Annuity Trust can be set up in any number of different ways to accommodate your Estate Plan. For example, if you are not in need of a present income, but expect that you will spend significant sums on your child's education, you can set up a 20 year Annuity with your child as the Annuitant. This will get the child through college and probably be a great help should the child decide to start a family. Why have the child inherit property in later, high earning years rather than in the early, high expense/low income years?

☑ CREDITOR PROTECTION

If you keep the land and are sued, you could lose it to pay your creditors. If a beneficiary inherits the land, it could be lost to his creditors. But once the property is transferred to the Trust, the gift is made. Neither your creditors nor your beneficiary's creditors can gain access to the Trust funds. The most a creditor can do is seek payment from the money that is received as an income.

☑ GOOD DEED

If you are concerned that your son will be tagged with a Capital Gains Tax once you die, it means that your property has appreciated more than 1.3 million dollars, and you are fortunate indeed. By setting up a Charitable Trust, you are making a donation to the charity of your choice. You are sharing your good fortune with others. You can consider this as "giving back" to the community, or just plain doing a good deed.

BECOME A PHILANTHROPIST

Instead of giving the property to an established charity, you can become a philanthropist and set up your own Charitable foundation. The foundation can be in the form of an IRS approved Charitable Trust. You can be the Trustee of the Charitable Trust and your child the Successor Trustee. The Trust can be set up according to your specific charitable purposes. You can use the Trust to benefit a single cause or several worthy projects. This can be an exciting adventure for those with ample resources and a community spirit.

An Estate Plan For Your Person

The law makes a distinction between your property (what you own) and your person (your body). We have been discussing how to set up an Estate Plan for your property with the goal of maximum control over your Estate during your lifetime, and minimum cost and hassle to your heirs once you die. An Estate Plan for your body is just as important as an Estate Plan for your property. The goals are much the same. Maximum control over your body during your lifetime. Minimum cost and hassle to your family for your final disposition.

You may think it strange to speak of planning for maximum control of your body during your lifetime. After all, it's your body. Who else but you has any right to control what you do with your body? That may be true so long as you have capacity, but should you become seriously ill, you may be unable to express your wishes about the care you wish to receive. If you do not have an Estate Plan in place for your person, then your next of kin, or maybe the state of Virginia may make health decisions for you.

The same applies to the final disposition of your body. Virginia courts have ruled that if you don't make burial or funeral arrangements, those decisions will be made by your Personal Representative or your surviving spouse or your next of kin (*Grisso v. Nolen*, 554 S.E. 2nd 91 (Va 2001)).

As this chapter will show, it is relatively simple and inexpensive to set up an Estate Plan for your Person.

MAKING BURIAL ARRANGEMENTS

People with a large family often arrange for a family burial site. Over the years deceased family members come to occupy a space in that site, but others may have been buried elsewhere. Surviving family members often lose track of the number of spaces left. If this is the case with your family, then you need to take inventory of the number of spaces available and who in the family expects to use those spaces.

It is important to keep in touch with the cemetery and let them know if there is a change in the expected occupant of the burial site.

OUT OF STATE BURIAL SITE

It may be that the family burial site is not in the state of Virginia. In such case, it is important to consider the cost of transporting the body from Virginia to the out-of-state cemetery. That cost can be substantial, in some cases doubling the cost of the burial. If there is no emotional attachment to the out-of-state burial site, you may want to consider assigning the burial site to a family member who lives closer to the site and making your own burial arrangements here in Virginia.

It is important to make your own burial arrangements. Even if it is not important to you where you are buried, it may be very important to your family. That is often the case in second marriages. If you have children from a first marriage, they may want their parents to be "reunited in death." Your current spouse may not take kindly to having you buried with your former spouse. This might result in hard feelings, if not an out-and-out battle.

The same problem can arise with those in a gay relationship. The decedent's family might not have acknowledged the relationship. The family might decide to have the decedent buried in the family plot and exclude the gay partner from participating in the burial arrangements.

You can head off disputes about your final resting place, by making your own burial arrangements.

ARRANGING FOR CREMATION

Increasingly people are opting for cremation. The reasons for choosing cremation are varied, but for the majority, it is a matter of finances. The cost of cremation is approximately one-sixth that of an ordinary funeral and burial. A major saving is the cost of the casket. A casket is not necessary for the cremation. An alternate container of fiberboard or similar materials, can be used to transport the body. Embalming is not necessary either, unless there is to be a funeral with a viewing. Federal law prohibits a funeral director from saying that a casket or embalming is necessary for a direct (immediate) cremation (16 Code of Federal Regulations ("CFR") 453.3 (b)(1)(ii)).

For those who are considering cremation, there are a few things to consider.

THE OVERWEIGHT
Cremation may not be an option for those who weigh more than 300 pounds. Many cremation services do not have the facilities to handle a large body. If you weigh more than 300 pounds, you need to check with your local cremation service to determine whether this will be a problem.

THE PACEMAKER

Cremating a body with a pacemaker or any radiation producing device can cause damage to the cremation chamber and/or to the person performing the cremation. If you have such an electronic aid, it will need to be removed prior to the cremation. You might check with the cremation service to determine the cost of having the pacemaker removed.

A pacemaker can be donated for use in animals with a medical need for the service. If you are interested in making such donation, you can ask your local veterinarian to refer you to an animal clinic that performs the procedure, and then arrange to have it removed prior to your burial or cremation.

WHAT TO DO WITH THE ASHES

In addition to planning for the procedure, you need to give your family some guidance as to where to place the ashes. Some cemeteries allow an urn containing the cremated remains of a family member to be placed in an occupied family plot. Similarly, some cemeteries will allow the cremated remains to be placed in the space in a mausoleum that is currently occupied by a member of the decedent's family. If you intend to be cremated and all your family spaces are occupied you may want to call the cemetery and ask them to explain their policy as it relates to the burial of urns in occupied sites.

If burial in the family site is not an option, you will need to arrange for a separate burial space. Many cemeteries have a separate building called a *columbarium*, which is especially designed to store urns. You can purchase a storage place for the urn in the same manner as the purchase of a burial space in a cemetery.

If you wish to have your cremated remains scattered, you need to let your next of kin know where and how this is to be done. If you want your ashes spread out to sea, your family will need to arrange to have a boat go out at least three nautical miles, because federal law prohibits ashes from being scattered any closer than that distance from land (40 CFR 229.1).

THE MILITARY BURIAL

If you are an honorably discharged veteran or the spouse of the veteran, you have the right to be buried in a Veterans National Cemetery. If your Veteran spouse was buried in a Veterans National Cemetery, you have the right to be buried in that same grave site unless soil conditions require a separate burial site. You can get information about military burials at a Veterans National Cemetery by calling the Veteran's Administration at (800) 827-1000, or by visiting their Web site.

VA CEMETERY WEB SITE
http://www.cem.va.gov

You cannot reserve a grave site in advance, so your family will need to make arrangements and establish your eligibility to be buried in a Veterans National Cemetery. At such time, they will need to provide the following information:

➤ your rank, serial, social security and VA claim numbers

➤ the branch of service in which you served; the date and place of your entry into and separation from the service

➤ a copy of your official military discharge document bearing an official seal or a DD 214 form.

You need to make this information available to the person who will see to your burial.

THE PREARRANGED FUNERAL

If you are financially able, in addition to arranging a burial space, consider purchasing a Preneed Funeral Plan. It will be easier on your family emotionally and financially if you make your own funeral arrangements. Federal law requires that you receive a general price list at the beginning of any discussion for the purchase of funeral services (16 CFR 453.2). Once you decide upon a plan, the seller should give you a contract that states the prices charged for *services* (embalming, viewing, transportation, etc.) and *merchandise purchased* (casket, urn, acknowledgment cards, register books, flowers, clothing, etc.) and *cash advance items*; i.e. things paid for by the funeral director and then reimbursed back to him. This includes paying for death certificates, arranging to have the obituary printed, payment for religious services, etc. (16 CFR 453.5).

In addition to federal law, Virginia law 54.1-2820 requires that the seller use a form prepared by the Virginia Board of Funeral Directors and Embalmers. The form should contain the Board's address and telephone number.

Even though the seller gives you a standard contract, it does not mean that it cannot be changed. If you are not satisfied with the way a certain section of the contract reads, then attach an addendum to the contract that explains, in plain English, your understanding of that passage. If you are concerned about something that is not mentioned in the contract, then insist that the contract be amended to include that item.

In particular, check to see whether the contract answers the following questions.

Does the contract cover all costs?

The contract should contain an itemized list stating exactly what goods and services are included in the sales price. Your contract may include an allowance towards cash advance items such as the printing of the obituary or payment to the clergy, or your contract may provide that payment be made at the time of the funeral. Your contract should state that the amount charged by the funeral director for a cash advance item be no more than the amount paid by the director for that item.

Is the price guaranteed?

Some Preneed Funeral Plans have a fixed price for the goods and services you choose, meaning that the funeral director will provide the goods and services at the same price as agreed at the time of the contract. It is important that your contract state that the person or company who is selling you the Funeral Plan is the same person or company who will actually provide those goods and services. If not, Virginia law requires the seller to attach to your contract, his agreement with the company that is actually going to provide the goods and services (VA 54.1-2820 (A) 10). You may want to read such an agreement to be sure that the provider has agreed to honor your contract.

You might opt for a Preneed Funeral Contract that is not a fixed price; meaning that the company can charge additional monies for the plan that you chose upon your death. In these days of an ever increasing life expectancy, it is important that such a contract clearly state how the price will be determined when the contract is finally put into effect.

How are your contract funds protected?

You can fund your plan by purchasing a life insurance policy. Virginia law requires that the face value of the policy be adjusted each year in accordance with the U.S. Consumer Price Index — or — the monies payable at death must equal the amount of monies paid for the policy, plus interest, which for the first 15 years must be at least 5% compounded annually. The law also requires that the relationship between the seller of the contract, the company that is going to provide the goods and services, and the insurance company be made known to you (VA 54.1-2820 B). If they are all one and the same, you may want to consider purchasing an insurance policy from an independent insurance company.

You may decide to pay cash for your Preneed Funeral Plan. In that case Virginia law requires that the funds be placed in a Trust account in a bank in the state of Virginia. If you have a guaranteed price contract, then 90% of the monies paid must be placed in the Trust account. If you do not have a fixed priced contract, 100% of the monies you pay must be placed in the Trust account. The funds must be deposited within 30 days. You may want to have your contract state that you will be provided with proof of deposit.

Virginia law gives you the right to choose the Trustee of the account. The law allows the funeral home to serve as Trustee, provided the funds cannot be removed unless there are at least two different Trustees who must act jointly to remove the funds (VA 54.1-2822). However, there are things you need to consider:

INTEREST IS INCOME TO YOU

Because you own the account, interest on that account will be included as taxable income to you.

SERVICE FEE

The funeral firm and or the bank may charge an initial service fee as well as an annual service fee. You need to determine how much will be charged. Your contract should state the amount that will be charged, and whether you will forfeit the initial and annual service fee should you decide to cancel your contract (VA 54.1-2820(A)(5)).

Can you cancel the contract?

Virginia law gives you the right to cancel your Preneed Funeral Contract at any time. If you revoke the contract within 30 days of signing the contract, you have the right to receive all of your monies back (plus interest) if the funds were placed in a Trust account.

After 30 days the amount you will receive back depends on the terms of the contract. Virginia law requires that you receive all of the monies in the Trust account, but in a guaranteed price contract, only 90% of the funds are deposited, so at the very least you will forfeit 10% of what you paid (VA 54.1-2820 (A)(7)).

Is the funeral firm reputable?

All these precautions don't do much good if you are not dealing with a reputable company. It is important to take the time to check up on whoever is selling you the contract. In Virginia, anyone who offers Preneed Funeral Plans to the public must be licensed to do so. You can check to see if the seller is licensed by calling the Board of Funeral Directors and Embalmers at (800) 533-1560. Out of state, call (804) 662-9907. You may also want to ask how long they have been in business and whether any complaints have been filed against them.

It is important to read and understand that part of the contract that deals with your right to revoke the contract and get your money back. If you are using an insurance policy to fund the plan, you need to know how much you will lose should you cancel the insurance policy. If you intend to pay for your Funeral Contract on an installment basis, you need to know how much of the monies you pay will be returned to you in the event that you default on payment.

FUNERAL PLANS FOR THOSE ON PUBLIC ASSISTANCE
People who are applying for, or receiving, Medicaid, Supplemental Security Income ("SSI") or other public assistance program have limits on the amount of assets that they own. If someone purchases a Preneed Funeral Plan, the monies paid into the plan count as an asset because the purchaser of the plan can revoke the contract and get his money back. The money he paid for the Funeral Plan might place the applicant over the asset limit. Understanding the problem, the Virginia legislature passed a law that allows the applicant to pay for the plan by placing the funds in an irrevocable Preneed Funeral Trust (VA 54.1-2820 (A7), 55-19.5). The Trust must be drafted according to Virginia law, so it will take the assistance of an Elder Law attorney to draft the document.

If you are in the process of applying for a public assistance program, before finalizing your funeral plan, it is prudent to check with your local Department of Social Services to be sure that your plan will not affect your ability to qualify for the program. Even if you are in good health at this time, it is a good idea to have your contract provide that you can change your plan to conform to state and federal law, if at any time you need to apply for a public assistance program.

Suppose you die in another state or country?

Your contract should spell out what provision will be made in the event that you move to another state or die in another state or country. Many funeral firms are part of a national funeral service corporation with funeral firms located throughout the United States. You may be able to have the contract provide that there will be no additional charge if the contract is performed by one of the funeral firms owned by the parent company.

Can the plan be changed after your death?

It may happen that your heirs need to cancel the plan after your death because:

➢ your body is missing or cannot be recovered, or

➢ you were buried by another facility because no one knew that you had a Preneed contract, or

➢ you died in another country and were buried there.

Your contract should address these potential problems, and spell out how much money will be refunded and who is to receive the refund.

You may also want to specify whether your heirs have the right to alter your funeral plans. In the absence of such a provision in the contract, funeral firms usually allow the family to arrange for a more expensive plan, provided they agree to pay the difference.

You may wonder why anyone would think of changing the decedent's funeral plan, but consider that in today's market, it is not uncommon for a Preneed Funeral Plan to cost several thousand dollars. A top end funeral complete with solid bronze casket can cost upwards of $40,000. Some heirs might be motivated to save money by changing the plan to one of a lesser value.

That was the case with Lester. His mother, Mona, was a difficult woman with a personality that can only be described as "sour." Her husband deserted her after four years of marriage leaving her to raise Lester by herself. Once Lester was grown, Mona made it clear to him that she had done her job and now he was on his own. Lester could have used some help. He married and had three children. One of his children suffered with asthma and it was a constant struggle to keep up with the medical bills.

Mona believed in being good to herself. She did not intend to, nor did she, leave much money when she died. She knew that Lester would not be able to afford a "proper" burial for her, so she purchased a funeral plan and paid close to $18,000 for it. She was pleased when the funeral director told her that the monies would be kept safely in a Trust account until the time they were needed.

Lester was not familiar with Virginia law, so when Mona died he asked an attorney at the Legal Aid office to determine whether the Preneed contract was revocable.

It was.
You know the ending to this story.

The reader might be thinking "Revocable. Irrevocable. All this contract stuff is giving me a headache. Why can't I just set aside some money and let my kids figure it out?"

The problem with that approach is that the cost of your final illness may leave you with little or no funds for your burial. To avoid the problem, you could purchase a life insurance policy to fund your funeral and burial, naming one or two trusted family members as the beneficiary of the policy. It is important that the person who is to receive the insurance funds clearly understands why he/she is named as beneficiary of the policy.

It isn't so much that a family member is not trustworthy as it is that they may not understand what you intended — especially in those cases where other funds are available to pay for the funeral. Too often insurance funds are left to a child who refuses to contribute to the cost of the funeral saying "Dad wanted me to have this money. That's why he left it to me." To avoid a misunderstanding, put it in writing. It need not be a formal contract. It could be something as simple as a letter to the insurance beneficiary, with copies to your next of kin. For example:

Dear Paul,

*I purchased a $20,000 insurance policy today naming you as beneficiary of the policy.
As we discussed this money is to be used to pay for the following:*
- my funeral; grave site and headstone
- perpetual care for my grave
*- airfare for each of my grandchildren
   to attend the funeral*
- dinner for the family after the wake
- lunch for the family after the funeral

If there is any money left over, please accept it as my thanks for all the effort spent on my behalf.
Love,
  Dad

*P.S. I am sending a copy of this letter to your
      sister so that she will know that all
      arrangements have been made.*

ANATOMICAL GIFT

Whether or not you arrange to pay for your burial or funeral, you need to let your next of kin know your feelings about the burial procedure. Let your family know whether you wish to be cremated or buried. If you wish to have a religious service, let your family know the type of service and where it is to be held. Let the family know where you wish to be buried, or if you intend to be cremated, where to place the ashes.

If you want to make an anatomical gift to take effect upon your death, you can make the gift as part of your Will; but it may be some time before your Will is located. The better route is to make the donation by a separate writing. You can complete an organ donor card when you apply for your Virginia driver's license or Virginia Photo Identification Card. If you do not want the fact that you are an organ donor indicated on your driver's licence or Photo ID, you can sign a donor card and give it to a trusted family member. Virginia statute 54.1-2984 contains a form that you can complete to make the donation. You can download the statute from the Virginia statute Web site: http://www.state.va.us

GIFT FOR EDUCATION AND RESEARCH
There is no age limit on organ and tissue donations, however doctors will probably not consider your body suitable for transplantation if you are of advanced age and in poor health. You can still donate your body to a school of medicine or dentistry for education and research. If you wish to make such a donation you can call the Virginia State Anatomical Program (804) 786-2479 and they will send you information about making the donation.

Schools generally pay for local transportation of the body to the school. There could be a substantial transportation cost should you die far from the school, so you need to give your family instructions about what to do should that happen. Similarly, schools will not accept a donation if the person was obese or died from a contagious disease, or a crushing injury, so you need to make alternate provision for such events.

If you do not wish to make an anatomical gift, then let your family know how you feel. If you do not make provision for a gift, and do not tell anyone how you feel about donating any or all of your body, the decision will be up to your family. Virginia statute states an order of priority for those who can give permission to make an anatomical gift:

1st the person you appointed as your Health Care Agent

2nd your spouse

3rd an adult child

4th either of your parents

5th a grandparent

6th your Court appointed Guardian, if any.

When permission is obtained from a family member and there are others in the same or a higher priority, then an effort must be made to contact those people and make them aware of the proposed gift. For example, if the sister of the decedent agrees to the gift (4th in priority) and the decedent had an adult child (2nd in priority), the child needs to be made aware of the gift. If the child objects, no gift can be made. Similarly, the statute prohibits the gift if, just before he died, the decedent said he did not want to make a donation (VA 32.1-290.1).

AUTOPSIES

An autopsy is one of those things that most of us do not think about; reasoning that if it is needed, it will be carried out and, being dead, you will have no choice in the matter. But there are many times when an autopsy is optional. Sometimes a doctor is not sure of the cause of death, and asks the family to allow an autopsy. It is often in the family's best interest to consent to the autopsy. The examination might reveal a genetic disorder, that could be treated if it later appears in another family member. Death from a car "accident" could have been a heart attack at the wheel. Perhaps the patient who died suddenly in a hospital was misdiagnosed. The nursing home resident could have died from negligence and not old age. Even if none of these are found, knowing the cause of death with certainty is better than not knowing.

Virginia law gives an order of priority to give authorization for the procedure:
1st   anyone you authorized, in writing,
       to dispose of your body
2nd   your spouse   3rd   your adult son or daughter
4th   either parent   5th   an adult brother or sister
6th   your Court appointed Guardian, if any
7th   anyone authorized to dispose of the body.
No authorization can be made if someone with the same or higher priority objects to the examination (VA 54.1-2825, 54.1-2973).

The person giving authorization must agree to pay for the autopsy because the cost is not covered under most health insurance plans, and it can cost several hundred to thousands of dollars. If you have strong feelings one way or another, then it is important to let your family know whether you would want an optional autopsy.

Of course, there are problems with just telling someone how you feel about your burial arrangements, autopsies, and anatomical gifts:

YOU TELL THE WRONG PERSON

You may tell someone who does not have authority to carry out your wishes. That was the case with James. When his wife died, he moved to a retirement community where he lived for several years until his death. James had two sons who lived in different states. Although he loved his sons, he had difficulty talking to either of them about serious matters. It was easier for him to talk with his friends in the retirement community. They often spoke about dying and how they felt about different burial arrangements. James would reminisce about his youth and growing up in a farming community in the plains state of Kansas. "I was happy and free. Out there you had room to breathe. It would be nice to be buried there — peaceful and spacious."

When he died, his friends told his sons about their father's desire to be buried in Kansas. They met the suggestion with scepticism and pragmatism:

"Dad didn't say anything like that to me."

"It would cost us double, if we had to arrange for burial in another state. I'm sure he didn't have that kind of expense in mind."

THE PERSON DOES NOT CARRY OUT YOUR WISHES

Sometimes the person you tell about the disposition of your body may not understand what you said or perhaps they hear only what they want to hear. Whether they follow your burial instructions or authorize an autopsy or an anatomical gift may depend more about what costs are involved, and their own feelings, rather than what you may have wanted.

Even if you tell someone and trust that person to carry out your wishes, it could be that the person you confide in cannot carry out your instructions. For example, if you tell your spouse what arrangements to make, he/she may become incapacitated or die before you do; or perhaps you both die together in a natural disaster or in a plane crash.

WHO WANTS TO TALK ABOUT IT?

For many people the main problem with telling someone what to do when you die is talking about your death. It may be an uncomfortable, if not unpleasant, subject for you to bring up, and for your family to discuss. If this is the case, then consider putting the information in writing and give the instructions to the person who will have the job of carrying out your wishes.

Making provision for the disposition of your body is important, but it is more important to make sure that you are in control of the health care you receive should you become seriously ill. This is not a problem when you are well enough to make your own medical decisions; however it could happen that you are too ill to let people know what you want.

The solution to the problem is to appoint someone, a **HEALTH CARE AGENT**, to carry out your directions about the disposition of your body. You can appoint an Agent by signing a document called an **ADVANCE MEDICAL DIRECTIVE**. The Advance Medical Directive can be used to make arrangements for the disposition of your body. More importantly you can use the Advance Medical Directive to give your Health Care Agent authority to make decisions about your health care during your life time in the event that you are too ill to do so yourself.

APPOINTING A HEALTH CARE AGENT

Virginia statute 54.1-2984 contains a statutory form that you can use to appoint a **Health Care Agent** to make your medical decisions in the event that you are too ill to do so yourself.

The statutory form contains a **Living Will** that tells your Health Care Agent whether you do (or do not) want life support systems to be used in the event that you are dying and there is no hope for your recovery. If you want to make an anatomical gift, you can give your Health Care Agent authority to consent to the gift on your behalf. If you do not wish to make an anatomical gift, then you can direct your Health Care Agent not to allow the procedure.

You can prepare your own Advance Medical Directive by copying the statutory form of the Advance Medical Directive. You can look up the statute by going to the nearest courthouse law library. You can also download the form from the Internet: http://www.state.va.us

You can have your attorney prepare an Advance Medical Directive especially designed to meet your special needs. For example, you can include funeral or burial arrangements as part of your Advance Medical Directive (VA 54.1-2825). It makes more sense to put these instructions in your Medical Directive rather than in your Will. Your Will may not be found for several days after your death, but your Advance Medical Directive is available to your Health Care Agent as soon as it is signed.

If you do not appoint someone to act as your Health Care Agent and you are too sick to make your own medical decisions, then the person with priority to make your medical decisions is established by Virginia statute:

1st   your Court appointed Guardian (if any)
2nd your spouse
3rd an adult child
4th   a parent
5th   an adult brother or sister
6th   any other relative in descending
        order of blood relationship
        (VA 54.1-2986).

A person with priority must be reasonably available, willing and competent to make medical decisions for you. If not, the next one with priority will make the decision. If there are several people with equal authority and they disagree about the proposed treatment, the statute authorizes the doctor to follow the direction of a majority.

If this order of priority is not as you wish, or if there is someone you wish to exclude altogether from making your health care decisions, then it is important to sign an Advance Medical Directive and appoint the person of your choice to act as your Health Care Agent. If not, life decisions made for you, may not be as you would have wished.

George is a case in point. He was a devoted husband and father. His wife came down with Alzheimer's disease. George cared for her at home, but finally it was too much for him and he had to place her in a nursing home. He and his daughters often visited, although she scarcely recognized them.

George met Emily during one of his visits. Her husband also suffered from Alzheimer's and was a resident of the nursing home. George and Emily had much in common. After visiting with their respective spouses, they would go to the local coffee shop. One thing led to another and soon they were an item.

George's daughters were not happy with his "lady friend." They criticized everything about her — from the way she dressed, to her table manners. Emily did not take it personally. She believed the girls were more interested in their expected inheritance, than George's happiness. A second marriage might cut into what they considered to be rightfully theirs.

Not that George and Emily planned to wed. They both loved their respective spouses and had no intention of trying to obtain a divorce. They just enjoyed each other's company. Caring for their respective spouses , they learned to take it one day at a time. That philosophy carried over into their relationship. They were both content to enjoy social outings with each other — dinner, movies, playing golf, and so on.

Both were happier than they had been in years. But that happiness was short-lived. George suffered a stroke while driving a car. He was seriously injured and lapsed into a coma. The prognosis was not encouraging. The doctors said George would die unless they put him on a ventilator and inserted a feeding tube. Even with these life support systems, they were not promising that he would survive.

Emily pleaded to keep him alive. "Let's try everything. If he doesn't improve, we can always discontinue the life support systems later."

George's daughter did not see it that way. "Why torture him with needles and tubes. Let him pass on peacefully."

George never signed a Living Will, so no one knew how he felt about life support systems. He never appointed anyone to be his Health Care Agent to make his medical decisions when he was unable to do so himself. In the absence of an Advance Medical Directive, the doctors followed Virginia law. George's spouse had priority to direct his treatment however because she was unable to do so, his daughters had the right to make his medical decisions.

Emily had no legal authority to direct his treatment.

George died.

A Health Care Estate Plan 9

We discussed an Estate Plan as it relates to the distribution or management of your Estate once you are deceased. In this age of extended life expectancy, a more pressing concern is how to manage and preserve your Estate in the event of a debilitating illness. As life expectancy increases, so does the percentage of the population who suffer incapacitating strokes, Alzheimer's disease or Parkinsons' disease. It is estimated that more than half of the population who are 85 or older, have some degree of dementia. Your best Estate Plan could be sabotaged by a lengthy illness. In this chapter we will explore ways to pay for the health care that you may require as you age.

In addition to paying for your health care, you need to consider who will care for your finances and everyday physical needs in the event that you are too ill to do so yourself. A **Health Care Estate Plan** is a plan designed to care for your person and property in the event of an incapacitating illness. In the last chapter, we discussed how you can appoint a Health Care Agent to care for your person in the event of your incapacity.

But there is still the problem of who will care for your property. In this chapter we will discuss how you can appoint someone to care for your property and manage your finances in the event of your incapacity.

The optimum way to provide for the care of your property in the event of your incapacity is to set up a Trust appointing a Successor Trustee to care for your property according to the directions given in your Trust. You can be Trustee of the funds while you have capacity. Should you become incapacitated, then the person you name as Successor Trustee will take over. But if you do not have sufficient assets to justify the cost of employing an attorney to draft a Trust, then there are other strategies you can use to solve the problem.

THE JOINT ACCOUNT

You can set up a joint checking account so that a trusted family member can write checks on the account. Of course there are all the inherent problems of a joint account that we discussed in Chapter 2. You can avoid many of those problems by limiting the amount of money that can be accessed by the family member. For example, you can arrange your finances so that all of your bills are paid from a single checking account and your family member can access that account, only.

If you set up a joint account, your family member will own whatever is in the account should your die. If this is not as you wish, you can instruct the bank that this is a *Convenience Account* and that in the event of your death the family member may no longer access your account. But ultimately the family member must be trustworthy because the bank is under no duty to stop your family member from writing checks on your account until the bank learns of your death.

The joint or convenience account solves the problem of how to pay your bills in the event you are temporarily ill. It does not solve the problem of how to manage your business affairs in the event of an extended illness. For example, suppose you have a stroke and can no longer be cared for at home. Should it be necessary for you to sell your home and move to an assisted living facility, no one will have the authority to sell the house for you. In such case, your friends or family members may be forced to ask the Court to appoint a Conservator to manage your finances, and if you did not appoint a Health Care Agent, a Guardian to make your medical decisions and care for your person.

The Court will set a competency hearing and will appoint a Guardian Ad Litem to protect your interests at the hearing. The Guardian Ad Litem will visit you and explain your rights under Virginia law. You can have your own attorney represent you at the hearing. If you do not have an attorney, the Court can appoint one for you. Determining whether you have capacity to take care of yourself can be an embarrassing, and demeaning experience, if you are sufficiently aware of the proceedings. You may want to employ an attorney to fight the matter.

If it is determined that you are incapacitated, the Court will appoint a Conservator and/or a Guardian. If a Conservator is appointed he will take possession of your assets and file an inventory with the Court. Each year he will account to the Court for monies spent. The Court may decide that a bond is necessary to protect your assets and order your Conservator to obtain a bond (VA 37.1-134.9, 37.1-134.12, 37.1-134.13, 37.1-137.2).

If a Guardian of your person is appointed, he will see to your health care. He will need to prepare and file a report each year regarding your well-being. The Guardian will need to employ an attorney to establish the Guardianship and to see that reports are properly and timely filed.

The Guardian and the Conservator (and their attorneys) are entitled to reasonable compensation for these services. Even if the same person serves as Guardian and Conservator, and there is only one attorney, the cost to your Estate is sizable (VA 37.1-134.16, 37.1-137.2).

Court filing fees, the Guardian Ad Litem fee, the cost of a bond, your attorney's fees, accounting fees, Conservator and Guardian fees, and their attorney fees, all are paid from your Estate (that's your money!).

Conservatorship and guardianship procedures are expensive to set up and maintain. Curious that so many people worry about how to avoid Probate, when the greater concern should be how to avoid guardianship. Consider that it is not all that hard to arrange your finances so that no Probate is necessary. The cost to transfer your property to your beneficiaries should be minimal.

Even with a full Probate procedure, whatever it costs to Probate your Estate is a one-time expense. And Probate is a one-time procedure. Once monies are distributed to your beneficiaries, it is over. Not so if you become incapacitated. It can cost thousands of dollars to set up the Guardianship; and more money to care for you and your property each year. And this expense goes on, year after year, until you are returned to capacity, or die.

As with Probate it is not all that hard to avoid these unnecessary charges to your Estate. To avoid the need for a Guardian of your person, you can appoint a Health Care Agent to make your medical decisions should you be too ill to do so yourself.

To avoid the need for a Conservator of your property, you can set up a Trust and appoint a Successor Trustee to care for your property in the event of your incapacity. For those of limited means, the **DURABLE POWER OF ATTORNEY** is the next best Estate plan.

A POWER OF ATTORNEY FOR FINANCES

A Power of Attorney is a legal document by which someone (the *Principal*) gives another (his *Agent* or *Attorney-In-Fact*) authority to do certain acts on behalf of the Principal. If you wish to have someone conduct business on your behalf in the event of your incapacity, you can make the Power of Attorney *durable* by adding the phrase "This Power of Attorney shall not terminate on the disability of the Principal" (VA 11-9.1).

You can give your Attorney-In-Fact general powers to manage your finances, to do much the same with your property as you can do yourself, such as:

⇨   sell any of your real or personal property;

⇨   buy real or personal property for you;

⇨   trade in securities;

⇨   pay your bills and/or taxes;

⇨   operate your business;

⇨   have access to your safe deposit box;

⇨   borrow money on your behalf;

⇨   purchase insurance policies and name beneficiaries;

⇨   sue or defend a law suit on your behalf;

⇨   apply for government benefits on your behalf.

You can even give your Attorney-In-Fact power to make gifts of your property in accordance with your Estate Plan, for example, you can direct him to give certain family members up to $11,000 in gifts each year (VA 11-9.5).

Notice that there are many things that your Attorney-In-Fact can do for you personally, such as defending a law suit or suing on your behalf or applying for government benefits. Even if you have a Trust, it is important to appoint an Attorney-In-Fact under a Durable Power of Attorney to do these important, personal, things for you, in the event you can't. Your Trust can only authorize your Successor Trustee to manage property that is placed in your Trust. Your Successor Trustee has no authority over you, personally. But you can give him (or anyone else) that authority by making him your Attorney-In-Fact under a Durable Power of Attorney.

GENERAL VS. LIMITED POWER OF ATTORNEY

You can sign a Power of Attorney giving your Agent broad general powers. With these powers your Agent can do much the same with your property as you can. Instead of a General Power of Attorney, you can limit the things your Agent can do with your property to just those things that you authorize in your Power of Attorney.

One power that should be specifically granted in your Power of Attorney, is the power to apply for medical assistance benefits in the event of your incapacity. In the next chapter we will be discussing the many things you can do to qualify for Medicaid. You need to give someone authority to take the necessary steps for you to become eligible for government benefits, in the event you are too ill to do so yourself. Even if you do not wish to give someone control over your finances at this time, you should give someone a Limited Power of Attorney for the purpose of qualifying for Medicaid.

Limited or General, the operative word in any Power of Attorney is POWER. Once your Attorney-In-Fact has authority to act, he essentially steps into your shoes and can do whatever you gave him authority to do. Your primary consideration in choosing an Agent is trustworthiness. You need to choose someone who will follow your instructions and put the Power of Attorney to the use you intended. You need to choose someone, who, when using your Power of Attorney, will always put your interests ahead of his.

You may be less concerned with trustworthiness than the loss of independence. But the thing to keep in mind is that you still have the power to do all of the things you gave your Attorney-In-Fact authority to do. The only difference is that now, you both have the power to conduct your business transactions.

Of course, shared authority is still less independent than sole authority; so you may hesitate to give someone a Power of Attorney until it is needed. But if you wait until it is needed, you may be too sick to sign the document. There are two simple solutions to this dilemma: keeping the document in your possession, or making it effective only upon you incapacity.

USING THE POWER OF ATTORNEY

An Attorney-In-Fact cannot operate on your behalf unless he has possession of the original Power of Attorney and presents it to whomever he wants to rely on that document. For example, if your Attorney-In-Fact wants to use the Power of Attorney to sell one of your securities, he will need to produce the original document and perhaps sign an Affidavit (a written statement sworn to before a Notary Public) saying that the Power of Attorney is still in effect and that you did not revoke that Power of Attorney.

KEEP THE DOCUMENT IN YOUR POSSESSION

Before anyone (a bank, stockbroker, closing agent, etc.) will accept the Power of Attorney, they will want to see the original document so that they are assured that your Attorney-In-Fact has authority to transact business on your behalf. If you keep the original document in your possession and do not give anyone a copy, your Attorney-In-Fact will not be able to act for you.

The only problem with this arrangement is that you need to arrange to make the document accessible to your Attorney-In-Fact in the event of your incapacity. If your Attorney-In-Fact is a trusted family member, then you can give him the location of the document with instructions to take possession of the Durable Power of Attorney in the event of your incapacity.

THE SPRINGING POWER OF ATTORNEY

A better solution may be to have your attorney draft a "springing" Durable Power of Attorney that is not operational until your family doctor and/or independent physician says that you are incapacitated and unable to manage your financial affairs. Your Attorney-In-Fact can hold the original document, but cannot use it until it "springs to life" when a doctor determines that you are too ill to care for your property (VA 11-9.4).

Your attorney can design a Durable Power of Attorney, to meet your special needs. He can even include powers that relate to your health care. But as a practical matter, it may be better to have a separate Advance Medical Directive. As explained in the previous chapter, the Advance Directive can be used to appoint a Health Care Agent and to give your Agent directions about the care you wish to receive in the event you are too ill to direct your medical treatment. There are two reasons to have a separate Advance Medical Directive:

APPOINT DIFFERENT PEOPLE TO SERVE

You may want one person to serve as your Health Care Agent and another to serve as your Attorney-In-Fact. One family member may be an excellent choice to make your health care decisions, yet that person may not be the best person to make financial decisions on your behalf.

PRIVACY

Even if you want the same person to serve as your Health Care Agent and Attorney-In-Fact, there is still the matter of privacy. Your Health Care Agent will give a copy of your Advance Medical Directive to your physician to be placed in your medical file. Your doctors have no need to know of your business dealings; and vice versa. To conduct business on your behalf, your Attorney-In-Fact will need to give a copy of the Power of Attorney to your business associates (banks, stockbrokers, etc.). Your business associates have no need to know of your medical decisions. For privacy, and perhaps security reasons, consider having a separate Advance Medical Directive for your health care and a Durable Power of Attorney for your finances, rather than try to get it all into a single multi-purpose document.

It is relatively simple and inexpensive to head off guardianship or conservatorship proceedings. All you need do is appoint an Attorney-In-Fact under a Durable Power of Attorney to manage your finances, and a Health Care Agent under an Advance Medical Directive to make your medical care decisions. These documents authorize people of your choice to care for you and your property in the event of your incapacity. But, despite your best plans, something unusual could happen causing a Court to decide that you need a Guardian or a Conservator. For example, suppose you disappear and cannot be found after a diligent search. It might be necessary to have a Court appoint a Conservator to protect your property in your absence. Or perhaps you develop an addiction or a mental illness causing self-destructive behavior. Your friends or family might decide that you are in need of protection and ask a Court to determine whether you are incapacitated, i.e., unable to care for yourself, and if so, appoint a Guardian to care for you (VA 37.1-134.8).

Although it may not be possible to avoid all guardianship and conservatorship proceedings, if you have appointed a Health Care Agent and an Attorney-In-Fact you can have some measure of control of your fate. Your Health Care Agent will continue to make your medical decisions in accordance with the directions given in your Advance Medical Directive. Your Attorney-In-Fact will continue to manage your finances in the manner you directed in your Power of Attorney. Whoever is appointed as Guardian cannot override the authority given in these documents unless he goes to Court and gets permission to do so. The judge will not revoke or modify your Medical Directive or Power of Attorney unless there is some pressing need to do so (VA 11-9.1, 37.1-137.1).

If you do not express your choice of Guardian, and two people want the job, both equally qualified, it will be up to the Court to decide who should care for you. In making the selection, he will be guided by your best interests; meaning that he will choose the person he thinks will do the best job in caring for you. However, some people look good on paper, but may be a poor choice. For example, suppose the Court finds that a woman is not capable of handling her finances and is need of a Conservator. If her son and daughter both want the job, the Court will consider their backgrounds and current commitments.

Suppose the son is a college graduate with a degree in business administration, and the daughter a homemaker with three small children. The judge might think the son a better choice, but it could be that the mother would never have chosen her son because of all the many times she had to bail him out of debt.

Again, it is a matter of planning ahead, and being in charge of your own destiny, rather than leaving the choice up to a judge to decide.

The good news is: You are going to live longer.
The bad news is: It's going to cost you.

Scientists are doing a great job of prolonging life, but unless they find Ponce De Leon's fountain, the general population will age. Along with age comes infirmities. Eyes fail. Hearing diminishes. Mobility declines. Digestive systems either speed up or slow down, all to the discomfort of the unhappy occupant of the body. It's all part of the "golden" years.

The pharmacology industry is well motivated to produce drugs that manage the ills associated with aging. Their research has led to a wealth of pharmaceutic products that do not cure, but do allow people to live in relative comfort into advanced age. The only problem is the cost of these drugs. Medicare covers the treatment of life-threatening brushes with heart disease, stroke, cancer and diabetes; but, as of this writing, Medicare does not pay for maintenance medication that is often necessary once the condition is stabilized.

Medicare is also limited in long term care coverage. It does not pay for extended nursing care. The federal government now offers a Medicare Advantage Plan and the Original Medicare Plan. With the Original Medicare Plan you do not pay for the first 20 days of skilled nursing care. You pay up to $109.50** per day for days 21 through 100. If you do not have Medicare Supplemental Insurance coverage, it will cost you up to $8,760 for the next 80 days.

**This is the value for the year 2005. The federal government adjusts the amount each year.

After 100 days, you are on your own. A nursing home stay of one or two years can wipe out the life savings of most working people. Once savings are gone, the government provides care in the form of Medicaid coverage.

If you have no assets to speak of, and a relatively low income, the cost of long-term nursing care is the least of your worries. Medicaid is available to take care of your medical and nursing care needs. And no need to worry if you are wealthy. You have enough money to pay for any care that you might need. The rest of us need to think about ways to provide for long-term health care.

For those concerned about the loss of life savings because of illness, there is supplemental and/or long-term health care insurance. There are many different insurance plans available. You can call the National Association of Insurance Commissioners at (816) 842-3600 and they will forward to you, free of charge, the publication:

A SHOPPER'S GUIDE TO LONG TERM CARE INSURANCE

If you have a specific question, you can call the Virginia Department of Aging at (804) 662-9333.

LONG TERM INSURANCE FOR FEDERAL EMPLOYEES

The Long Term Care Security Act (Public Law 106-265) was passed by Congress to take effect in October, 2002. The law is designed to make long term care insurance available to federal and postal employees, members of the uniformed services, civilian and military retirees, and their qualified relatives. You can call the Office of Personnel Management at (800) 582-3337 for information about the program or visit their Web site.

 OFFICE OF PERSONNEL MANAGEMENT
http://www.opm.gov/insure/ltc

The National Association Of Retired Federal Employees ("NARFE") has been actively involved in developing this legislation. You can get information about the program at the NARFE office in Alexandria, Virginia at (703) 838-7780 or from their Web site.

 NATIONAL ASSOC. OF RETIRED FEDERAL EMPLOYEES
http://www.narfe.org

THE PROBLEM OF COST AND ELIGIBILITY

Long term care insurance sounds like the perfect solution, until you start examining the cost. The cost isn't too bad if you are comparatively young, say in your 50s. But can you imagine paying that premium each month until you are in your 80s and never needing nursing care?

Many decide to wait till they are old and going downhill. But that just brings other problems. The older you are, the greater the cost of insurance. And there is the risk that you will be refused coverage because of a "pre-existing" condition, i.e., the insurance company may consider you to be too great a risk for them to insure.

Different insurance companies have come up with insurance plans that may provide a solution for the person who is relatively young and in good health. Some companies offer long-term care insurance that is paid-up within a fixed period of time. Once payments are made for a certain number of years, the person is insured for long-term care without further payment. Other companies combine long-term care insurance with a life insurance policy. They offer long-term care insurance that converts to a life insurance policy, if it happens that the insured person dies before needing long-term care. When shopping for a long-term care policy, consider including different insurance alternatives in your investigation.

WHEN INSURANCE IS NOT AN OPTION

For some people long term care insurance is not an option. An elderly person living on a low fixed income may not have enough money to pay the monthly premium for a long term care insurance policy. And long term care insurance is not an option for the person who has been diagnosed with a chronic, debilitating disease.

People in such a position worry that they may need to deplete their life savings, just to pay for a year or two of nursing care.

Both of these problems can be solved by using current law to become qualified for Medicaid. Medicaid is a public assistance program that is funded jointly by the federal and state government. There are state and federal laws governing who may become eligible for the program.

A *Medicaid Qualifying Plan* is a plan that takes both state and federal laws into consideration. Operating within the boundaries of these laws, those who are concerned about becoming impoverished in order to pay for long-term care, seek to preserve and protect their Estate by implementing a Medicaid Qualifying Plan.

There has been controversy about plans designed to qualify a person for Medicaid. Some think that to intentionally arrange finances to qualify for Medicaid is immoral — a legal method of working the system.

Those people may argue: "Why are such things allowed? After all, wasn't Medicaid designed to help <u>poor</u> people? Why should people be allowed to make themselves poor to get on the public dole??

Those who feel they need to qualify for Medicaid have a different point of view. They may argue:

"I worked all my life and hoped to leave a few pennies for the kids. Why did I work so hard? To give it all to a nursing home? I paid my taxes just like everyone else. The government pays hundreds of thousands of dollars for people on Medicare to have open heart surgery, and they pay for lengthy and expensive cancer treatments. Why should those who have Alzheimer's or Parkinsons or those who suffer a debilitating stroke, not be entitled to receive equal benefits?"

Although we can understand and appreciate both points of view, our job, as we see it, is to just explain the law as it is at the time of publication. We think it is important to do so because many people take a position (pro or con) based on what they perceive the law to be, and not based upon the law as it actually is.

Once the reader understands what it takes to qualify for Medicaid in the state of Virginia, he can decide for himself whether the law is basically fair to the people who need to qualify, or whether it is flawed (either too restrictive or too liberal) and needs to be changed.

Hopefully, those with a strong opinion will share those views with their legislators.

A Medicaid Qualifying Plan 10

A better name for this chapter might be "A Health Care Contingency Plan." A lengthy stay in a nursing home is something most of us do not want to even think about, much less prepare for. Why prepare for something that may never happen? Yet as we age, there is that nagging "What if?" "What if I need long term nursing care? How will I pay for it?"

An effective way to put this anxiety at rest is to have a contingency plan. To form a contingency plan, you need to know your options. In this case, your options are directly related to your ability to pay for that care. But it is hard to predict future fortunes. People win the lottery. Those with a large portfolio may have their fortunes disappear in a market melt-down. There is no need for concern if it turns you can afford to pay for your own nursing care. And there is no concern should you become impoverished because there are government programs that provide for your health care. The worst case scenario is that you will be able to afford long-term care, but at the cost of your life savings.

In this chapter we will discuss options available to you under that worst case scenario. We will explain current state and federal law as it relates to qualifying for medical assistance programs.

Once you know the law, you will be able to form a contingency health care plan that is right for you.

WHO IS ENTITLED TO MEDICAID?

Medicaid is a program that provides medical and long term nursing care for people with low income and limited resources. The program is funded and regulated by both federal and state government. The governing agency for the federal government is the Centers for Medicare and Medicaid Services. The Department of Medical Assistance Services is the state governing agency for the Medicaid program. In Virginia, Medicaid is part of the state's Medical Assistance Program. We will use the terms *Medicaid* and *Medical Assistance*, interchangeably.

Medicaid is an entitlement program, meaning that whoever qualifies for the program is entitled to receive benefits under that program. Applications are taken and the program administered at the local level by the Virginia Department of Social Services ("VDSS"). Those who do not qualify are not entitled to any Medicaid benefits.

There are many benefits offered under Medicaid, from health care for mothers and children; to community based services for those who need some assistance with their health care; to full nursing care for those who need assistance with dressing, bathing, eating, walking and toileting. We will limit our discussion of Medicaid to aged persons in need of institutional nursing care. You can get information about other Medicaid programs by calling your local Department of Social Services office. There is a list of local telephone numbers at the Virginia Department of Social Services Web site. The Web site also contains information about Virginia's medical assistance program.

 VIRGINIA DEPARTMENT OF SOCIAL SERVICES
http://www.dss.state.va.us

Persons who are receiving Supplemental Security Income ("SSI") may be automatically eligible for Medicaid because the requirements for these programs are much the same. If a person is not receiving SSI, he may be eligible for Medicaid if he is 65 or older, or blind, or disabled (VA 32.1-325).

When a person applies for Medicaid (the "Applicant"**) the VDSS will investigate his medical condition, income, and assets. If the Applicant is too ill to apply for himself, his spouse may apply for him (42 US Code of Federal Regulations ("CFR") 435.908). If the Applicant is single, his Agent under a Durable Power of Attorney, may apply for him, provided the Power of Attorney gives the Agent the authority to do so. If he did not appoint an Agent, it may be necessary to have a court appointed Conservator and/or a Guardian apply for Medicaid benefits on his behalf.

CITIZENSHIP ELIGIBILITY
To be eligible for Medicaid, the Applicant must be a resident of the United States, and either a U.S. citizen or a qualified alien who is lawfully admitted for permanent residence (42 U.S. 1396a, 1382c, 12 VAC 30-40-10).

MEDICAL ELIGIBILITY
The Applicant needs to be evaluated to determine whether he has a mental or physical condition that requires nursing supervision and assistance with activities of daily living. If the Applicant is not currently a resident of a nursing facility VDSS will have a staff member of an acute care hospital do a Pre-admission screening to determine whether the Applicant qualifies medically for the Medicaid nursing care program (VA 32.1-330).

** For simplicity, we will use the male gender for the Applicant and the female gender for his spouse.

INCOME ELIGIBILITY

In Virginia, there is no limit on the amount of income earned by the Applicant each month, because once he is approved his income will be used to pay for the cost of his nursing care. Of course should the Applicant have a very high income, there would be no reason to apply for Medicaid because he could afford to pay for his own nursing home care.

THE PERSONAL NEEDS ALLOWANCE

Once the Applicant is approved and becomes a recipient of Medicaid benefits (i.e. a *Medicaid Recipient*), his income will be used to supplement the cost of his nursing care. He will be allowed to keep a certain amount of his income each month (currently $30) for his personal needs, such as clothing or hair cuts (12 VAC 30-40-20).

RESOURCE ELIGIBILITY

Although there is no limit on the Applicant's income, there is a limit on his *Resources*. Resources are assets owned by the Applicant, either by himself or together with another, that are countable for purposes of qualifying for Medicaid. The Applicant may have no more than $2,000 in Resources. An Applicant who is over the Resource limit on the first day of the month that he applies for Medicaid needs to "spend down" his assets to $2,000. If he is eligible at any time during the month that he applies, his Medicaid benefits will begin on the first day of that month.

If the Applicant is married, he can transfer anything over $2,000 to his spouse, but there are limits to his spouse's assets as well.

THE COMMUNITY SPOUSE

The spouse of an Applicant who lives in their home or elsewhere in the community (i.e., not in a nursing home) is called the **Community Spouse**. Prior to 1988, the Community Spouse was required to use whatever assets she had to pay for the nursing care of her spouse. The Applicant could not quality for Medicaid until they both were virtually impoverished. In addition to being unfair to the Community Spouse, this was not good government policy because it often resulted in the impoverished spouse turning to local government social service programs for support.

The Medicaid provisions of the Medicare Catastrophic Coverage Act of 1988 remedied the situation by considering the assets of the couple as being part of a common pot and allowing the Community Spouse to keep her own share of that pot. The amount allowed has been increased over the years. The federal government currently allows the Community Spouse to keep up to $95,100 of their combined Resources.

The federal government also considers that the Community Spouse needs money each month for her maintenance. If her income is not sufficient to support her, the income of the Medicaid Recipient will be used to supplement the income of the Community Spouse up to a maximum of $2,377.50 per month. Each year, the federal government adjusts the spouse's Resource allowance and monthly maintenance allowance for cost of living increases. The value quoted are those used in 2005 (42 U.S.C. 1382b).

Notice that $95,100 and $2,377.50 are the maximum values as set by the federal government. States have the right to administer the Medicaid program according to their state law, provided their state law is within federal guidelines and does not exceed the maximum values set by the federal government. This being the case, the actual amount allowed to the Community spouse can vary significantly state to state.

The current value set by the state of Virginia, as the Community spouse's **Minimum Monthly Maintenance Needs Allowance** is $1,561.25. This includes $468.37 for shelter expenses (condominium maintenance fees, rent, mortgage, property taxes, homeowner's insurance, utilities etc.). If the spouse's shelter costs are greater than $468.37 the spouse is allowed an **excess shelter allowance**, provided the total value allowed as her monthly Needs Allowance does not exceed the current federal value of $2,377.50.

The Community Spouse is expected to contribute payment towards the care of the Medicaid recipient, provided her income is greater than $1,900. The VDSS will require the spouse to contribute $10 per month for every $100 over $2,000. Some examples might better explain these rules.

Suppose the Community Spouse's fixed income from Social Security, pension, etc. is $1,000 a month and VDSS determines that she needs a total of $1,600 each month for her maintenance. In such case, she will be allowed to keep $600 of her spouse's monthly income. She will not be expected to contribute anything toward his nursing care.

Suppose instead, her income is $2,500 per month. She is not entitled to any of the Medicaid recipient's income. All of it will be used to assist with the cost of his nursing care.

In addition, the Community Spouse must contribute $10 for each $100 over $2,000: $2,500 - $2,000 = $500

This means that she must contribute $50 each month for his nursing care: 5 x $10 = $50

THE SPOUSE'S RESOURCE ALLOWANCE

Assets owned by the Applicant, or his spouse, are considered to be available to the Applicant for purposes of Medicaid eligibility. Under federal law, the Community Spouse is entitled to keep a share of the couple's assets up to the current maximum of $95,100. That share is called the **Community Spouse Resource Allowance** (42 U.S.C. 1396r-5(c)(2), 1396r-5f).

In Virginia, the Community Spouse to allowed to keep half of their common pot of assets with a minimum value of $19, 020 up to the federal maximum value of $95,100. For example, suppose the couple own $20,000 between them. The Community Spouse is allowed to keep $19,020 as her Resource Allowance. The Applicant is allowed to keep the remainder as part of his $2,000 Resource Allowance. All other things being equal, the Applicant should qualify for Medicaid.

But suppose the couple have $150,000 worth of marital assets; i.e., property titled in either of their names. In that case, the Community spouse can keep her half ($75,000) as a Resource Allowance. The Applicant can keep his $2,000, but that leaves them with $73,000 above the limit.

The first question to ask in such a situation is whether all of their assets count as a Resource.

WHAT COUNTS AS A RESOURCE?

Property owned by the Applicant, and/or his spouse, that can be converted to cash and used for their support, are considered to be a Resource. This includes bank accounts, certificates of deposit, property in a Revocable Living Trust, stocks, bonds, and so on.

Some items owned by the Applicant, or his spouse, can be converted to cash, but are not counted as a Resource. Such items are considered to be "exempt assets" or "non-countable resources." We will refer to them as *Exempt Resources* (42 U.S.C. 1382b).

EXEMPT RESOURCES

The following items are Exempt Resources and do not count as a Resource for purposes of Medicaid Eligibility.

PERSONAL PROPERTY
Personal property being used by the Applicant or his spouse are exempt items. They include:
- ⇨ wedding and engagement rings, regardless of their value;
- ⇨ home furnishings and appliances, books, household tools

The VDSS will consider heirlooms, coin or stamp collections as personal property, provided they are not worth very much. Household items that are worth a significant amount of money, such as a valuable antique or an expensive painting, can be counted by the VDSS as a Resource.

LIFE INSURANCE

⇨ An insurance policy owned by the Applicant is exempt if the face value (the amount paid at death) is $1,500 or less. If the Applicant owns more than one policy on the same person, then they are exempt, provided that person is over age 21 and the sum of their face values is not greater than $1,500.

If the face value of the policy is more than $1,500, VDSS will count the Cash Surrender Value of the policy as a Resource (12 VAC 30-40-290).

BURIAL ARRANGEMENTS

⇨ Burial spaces for the Applicant or his family (spouse, child, parent, sibling and the spouse of a family member) are Exempt Resources. This includes prepaid burial space items such as grave sites, mausoleums, urns, niches, etc. Opening and closing the grave, headstones, and headstone engravings are also considered burial space items.

⇨ An Irrevocable Preneed Funeral Agreement as described in Chapter 8 is an Exempt Resource.

⇨ Burial funds up to $3,500 for the Applicant and $3,500 for his spouse are exempt, provided the fund is in a separate account and clearly identified as a burial account. This amount is reduced by the face value of a life insurance policy on the life of the Applicant or his spouse. It is also reduced by the amount paid for a Preneed Funeral Agreement for the Applicant or his spouse (12 VAC 30-40-290).

AUTOMOBILE

⇨ A car owned by the Applicant or his spouse is an Exempt Resource. If more than one car is owned, VDSS will exempt the most valuable car and count the value of the second (lesser valued) car as a Resource. VDSS uses the National Automobile Dealers Official Used Car Guide Book, Eastern Edition, to determine the value of the second car (12 VAC 30-40-290).

THE HOME

⇨ The primary residence (home, condominium, cooperative apartment, or mobile home) that is occupied by the Applicant or his family (spouse, minor or dependent child, dependent relative) is an Exempt Resource.

The Applicant's home is an Exempt Resource so long as it is his primary residence or that of a family member. If the Applicant is in a nursing home, and no family member lives in the home, it remains an Exempt Resource, provided the Applicant has indicated that he intends to return home, and it is expected that he will do so within 6 months. If this is not the case then his home counts as a Resource.

PENSION PLAN

⇨ The cash value of the Applicant's pension plan counts as a resource, but not if he is receiving a monthly distribution of the funds over his life expectancy. In such case, the pension funds are counted as income to the Applicant and will be used for his nursing care. The same applies to the Community Spouse's pension fund (including IRA's). If the spouse is receiving a monthly income based on her life expectancy, then VDSS counts this as income to the Community Spouse

INCOME PRODUCING PROPERTY

➪ The market or appraised value of property used in a trade or business may be excluded if it produces a reasonable rate of return. VDSS usually considers 6% to be reasonable.

ASSETS THAT ARE NOT SALEABLE

➪ Property owned by the Applicant or his spouse must be able to be converted to cash in order to be counted as a resource. Shares held in a close corporation, Life Estate interests, certain irrevocable annuities, and other non-saleable items can be considered as Exempt Assets, subject to the approval of the VDSS (12 VAC 30-40-290).

JOINTLY OWNED RESOURCES

The Department of Social Services considers the full value of a jointly owned asset to be available to the Applicant, or his spouse; unless it can be proven that the other owner contributed toward the property. For example, if the Applicant owns a joint account with his son, the entire balance counts as a Resource unless the son can prove that he contributed his own money to that account. The amount contributed by the son does not count as a Resource.

OTHER EXEMPT ASSETS

We listed common items that VDSS considers to be Exempt Resources. But this is not a complete list. There are other items that VDSS will not count as part of the Applicant's Resources. An experienced Elder Law Attorney will be able to examine all of the property owned by Applicant and tell him what assets the VDSS considers as exempt.

THE SPEND-DOWN OPTION

Now that we know what does (and does not) count as a Resource, the next question is what options are available to our couple who are over the Resource limit by $73,000. Those with no knowledge of the law, might think the only option available to this couple is to pay for his nursing care until the $73,000 runs out. Those who carefully read the previous pages, might suggest that the couple check to see whether they can use the money to purchase items that do not count as a Resource.

Both state and federal law allow the Applicant and his spouse to use their excess Resources to purchase items that are exempt, without losing the right to receive Medicaid benefits, provided they pay a fair market value for the item. This being the case, the couple can make funeral or burial arrangements, if they have not already done so. They can purchase household items such as furniture, a television set, a new refrigerator or stove, etc.

REPAIRING EXEMPT ITEMS
Paying money to repair an Exempt Resource is a good spend-down strategy. Perhaps the Exempt family car needs new brakes or tires. The Community Spouse may decide to replace the Exempt car with a new model.

If the house is in need of repair or improvement, this is the time to fix it up. A new heating, plumbing, electric or security or security system can use up funds quickly.

If the couple do not own their own home, the Community Spouse might consider using the excess cash as a down-payment on a home.

SPEND-DOWN BY TRANSFER TO DISABLED PERSON

As explained in Chapter 7, if a child is receiving Social Security disability benefits, the parent can transfer money to a Special Needs Trust for the child. This transfer will not disqualify the child, or the parent, from receiving government benefits, provided the Trust is drafted according to state and federal law. Before making the transfer it is important to check with VDSS to be sure they agree that the child is blind or disabled and that no penalty will be imposed for making such transfer (12 VAC 30-40-300).

SPEND-DOWN BY PAYING DEBTS

Some sceptics might think $73,000 is a lot of money to spend down. Maybe the couple previously made all funeral arrangements. Perhaps they really don't need (or want) new furniture or appliances. In such case, the solution may be to pay off all of their outstanding debts.

If the couple have a credit card balance, they can reduce the balance to $0. If their car is an Exempt Resource, they can pay off any money they may owe on the car. If they have a mortgage on their home, they can use the money to pay down that debt.

Paying off loans is a valid spend-down strategy because it is just a return of monies given to the Applicant by the lender for the purchase of an Exempt Resource (car, house, clothing, household items). But the Applicant will need to prove to the VDSS, that the monies he spent were used to pay off a valid debt. If he paid off a credit card debt, the VDSS will want to see the original contract with the company and the monthly bill showing what items were purchased. If a car loan was paid, the VDSS will want to see the original promissory note (marked "PAID"), as well as other loan items, such as a chattel mortgage.

If the money was used to pay down a mortgage on his home, VDSS will want to see the original loan documents as well as documents showing the new balance, or a satisfaction of mortgage, if it was paid in full.

 **TIMING IS IMPORTANT
WHEN SPENDING DOWN**

The couple's Resources are counted as of day that the Applicant began his first continuous period of institutionalization (42 U.S.C. 1396r-5(c)(A)). In most cases, this is the first day that the Applicant enters the nursing home. That date is called the ***Snap Shot Date*** because the VDSS takes a "picture" of their assets on that date. If the couple have $150,000 and a mortgage of $75,000 on the Snap Shot Date, he can apply for Medicaid at that time. The Community Spouse is allowed to keep half as her Resource Allowance ($75,000). The Applicant is allowed $2,000, so he is over the Resource limit by $73,000. He can use that money to pay down the mortgage, and be eligible for Medicaid the following month. This leaves the Community Spouse with $75,000 and an almost paid up mortgage.

Suppose instead that they pay the mortgage before the Snap Shot date. In that case, they will have $75,000 left. This leaves them in a worse position because VDSS will allow the Community Spouse to keep half of the $75,000 (only $37,500). The Applicant will be allowed to keep his $2,000, but he will be over the Resource limit by $35,500 and will need to spend down in some other manner. The same concerns arise when buying Exempt Resource or making repairs. If a married Applicant spends down before the Snap Shot Date, the Community Spouse may be left with less assets than if they had spent down after that date. Before using any spend down strategy, you may want to consult with an Elder Law attorney to determine the best course of action.

MAYBE SPEND-DOWN IS NOT NECESSARY

Suppose the couple with too much in Resources has too little income. For example, suppose it is determined that the Community Spouse needs at least $2,232 per month, but the couple's combined income is only $1,500. In such case, she can ask the VDSS to allow her to keep as much of couple's excess assets as is necessary to give her this minimum income. In effect, she needs to ask "May I keep more than my Resource Allowance so that the income from this property will help to get me to that minimum income?"

It is the legal right of the Community Spouse to receive the minimum income allowance allowed by both state and federal government. It is reasonable to ask the VDSS to allow her keep as much of their resources as is necessary to achieve that income, even if it means keeping more than allowed as a resource allowance.

In all probability the VDSS will deny the request and it will be necessary to go through an Appeals process to decide the issue. The Appeals process can drag on for months. Meanwhile, the status of the Applicant remains in limbo. Because of the legal cost of the Appeal and the uncertainty of whether the Court will agree that additional resources are necessary for the support of the Community Spouse, or whether this is a genuine case of undue hardship, it may be better to use a spend-down strategy that enables the spouse to obtain additional income.

One such strategy is the Medicaid Annuity. The Community Spouse uses her excess Resources to buy an Annuity that will give her additional income.

A spend-down strategy that is currently allowed by both federal and state law is the of purchase of *Immediate Pay Annuity*; i.e., an annuity whose payments begin the month after the purchase and continues for a fixed period of time. For purposes of Medicaid eligibility, that fixed period of time must be less than, or equal to, the life expectancy of the Annuitant (in this case, the Community Spouse). The life expectancy of the Annuitant is determined by referring to the actuarial table as published by the Centers for Medicare and Medicaid Services; State Medicaid Manual, Part 3 (SM3 3259.1) "Life Expectancy Tables—Males and Life Expectancy Tables—Females." You can find excerpts from that table at Public Service Information section of the Eagle Publishing Company Web site.

http://www.eaglepublishing.com

By purchasing an Immediate Pay Annuity, the excess Resources are converted to a monthly income that continues for the term of the policy.

In order to qualify as a permissible spend-down strategy, the Annuity must meet both state and federal criteria; specifically:

THE COMMONWEALTH IS THE RESIDUARY BENEFICIARY
The Annuitant is the primary beneficiary of the Annuity, but if the Annuitant dies before all payments are made, the remaining funds go to the state of Virginia up to the amount they spent for the care of the Applicant.

IRREVOCABLE

The Annuity contract cannot be transferred, sold or assigned. It must be irrevocable. In other words, nothing can be changed; not the monthly payment, nor the number of payments, nor the identity of the Annuitant or the Residuary Beneficiary (i.e., the state of Virginia).

EQUAL MONTHLY PAYMENTS

The money invested in the Annuity , plus interest, must be returned to the Annuitant during his life expectancy as printed in the State Medicaid Manual (SM3 3259.1)

There is no rounding "up." For example, according to the State Medicaid Manual a 65 year old man has a life expectancy of 14.96 years. An Annuity that makes regular payments to the Annuitant for 14 years is actuarially sound, but an Annuity that makes payments for 15 years is not.

The Annuity contract must be issued by an insurance company, bank, or other company licensed to do business in the county where the Annuity is issued.

We will refer to an Annuity that meets all of these criteria (Virginia as beneficiary, no cash value, unassignable, irrevocable, actuarially sound) as a *Medicaid Annuity*.

 VERIFY THAT THE ANNUITY MEETS
STATE CRITERIA PRIOR TO PURCHASE

Once the Annuity is purchased it is irrevocable, so before you buy it, have your Elder Law attorney, or the agent who is selling the Annuity, verify that the Annuity meets state and federal requirements.

If you purchase an Annuity and for some reason VDSS determines that it does not meet current state and federal criteria, they might consider the entire value of the Annuity to be an impermissible transfer of assets and a PENALTY PERIOD of ineligibility will be imposed, i.e., a period of time that the Applicant is disqualified from receiving Medicaid benefits. The Penalty Period is discussed later in this chapter.

Purchasing a Medicaid Annuity could solve the problem for the Community Spouse who has too little income and too much in Resources. She can use her excess Resources to buy the Annuity. She will keep the income from that investment, just as she would if she had invested in a stock, bond or Certificate of Deposit. Unlike these investments, part of the money she paid for the Annuity is returned to her each month along with interest. Most importantly, the Annuity does not count as a Resource.

This spend-down strategy can be used by the Community Spouse even when her income is not a problem. But it may not make economic sense if the sum of her monthly income, including the income from the Annuity, exceeds the amount determined by VDSS to be her Minimum Monthly Maintenance Needs Allowance. For example, suppose she needs $2,000 per month and her only income is $1,000 from Social Security. The VDSS allows her to keep $1,000 of her husband's income. If the Annuity pays $1,000 (or more), she may keep none of her husband's income. All of his income will be used for his nursing care.

In other words, purchasing the Medicaid Annuity may enable the Applicant to qualify for Medicaid, but it may not result in extra income for Community Spouse.

And there are other things to consider.

⇨ **ANNUITANT MIGHT DIE**

Should the Community Spouse Annuitant die before all monies are paid, the Commonwealth of Virginia becomes the beneficiary of Annuity up to the amount paid on behalf of the Recipient. It may be too much of an economic risk to purchase a Medicaid Annuity if the Community Spouse is in poor health.

⇨ **LOSS OF LIQUIDITY**

Should the Applicant dies shortly after she buys the Annuity, his Community Spouse cannot cash it in. She must keep the investment for the full term.

⇨ **RISK OF LOSS**

By purchasing an Annuity, the Community Spouse is giving her money to a company in exchange for the company's promise to return part of the principal each month, together with interest. The company promises to make these payments every month for a certain number of years. Should the company become bankrupt during that period of time, the monies invested might be lost.

⇨ **FIXED RETURN ON INVESTMENT**

Annuities offer a fixed rate of return on the money invested and there is no way to adjust that rate for periods of inflation. The rate of return on the Annuity is set at the time of purchase. We are currently in a period of low interest rates. Should there be a period of high interest rates, the Annuity will still yield the same rate of return as when purchased.

These concerns need to be addressed before investing in a Medicaid Annuity. Consultation with an Elder Law attorney prior to the purchase is a must.

Although purchasing a Medicaid Annuity may work for the Community Spouse with a low fixed income, it may not be the best strategy for the single Applicant, because any income he receives from the Annuity will be used for his nursing care. One exception may be the single Applicant who intends to return home after a few months.

For example, suppose a single father with $100,000 needs extensive nursing care because of a car accident. If doctors expect he will be able to return home after several months of therapy and nursing care, he might consider purchasing a Medicaid Annuity for $98,000.

Once he makes the purchase, he can immediately apply for Medicaid. He will of course report the purchase to VDSS. They will examine the terms of the Annuity to be sure they satisfy current regulations. If they do and he meets all other requirements, he should qualify for Medicaid.

He's happy because he did not need to spend down his $98,000 in nursing home bills. He's hoping that his condition improves enough so that he can return home. In such case, his nursing care will be paid by Medicaid, and he will continue to receive the income from the Annuity when he returns home.

The VDSS is happy because any income received while in the facility will go toward payment of the Recipient's nursing home bill; leaving that much less for the Commonwealth to contribute to his care. Should the Applicant die before his life expectancy, the Commonwealth will receive whatever monies remain in the Annuity up to the amount they paid for his nursing care.

Spend-down may not be the best strategy for the single Applicant with significant assets such as the father who has $100,000. Sure he can make his funeral arrangements; but that will only use up a small portion of his assets. He could buy an expensive car, but what good would that be if he needs to enter a nursing home? The Medicaid Annuity is a possibility, but if he has a progressive, long-term disease such as Alzheimer's or Parkinson, and needs to go into a facility, he could very well live longer than his life expectancy and all the money invested in the Annuity would be used for his care. Even if he dies before his life expectancy, the state will become the beneficiary of the Annuity up to the amount they contributed toward his care. It could happen that none of the money will go to his child.

If the Applicant has a medical condition that does not require immediate nursing care, he may decide to simply transfer all of his money to his child. The VDSS will consider this to be an *uncompensated transfer* i.e., the Applicant gets nothing in return for the transfer (love and affection don't count).

Should the Applicant go this route, he will be disqualified from receiving Medicaid for a period of time based on the amount that was transferred. The period of time that the Applicant is disqualified is called the *Penalty Period* or the *Period of Ineligibility.*

In Virginia, the rules regarding the Penalty Period are fairly complex. In general, they are computed by dividing the amount transferred by the average monthly cost of nursing home care as determined by the Department of Medical Assistance Services. The value varies depending on the location of the nursing home. The current value for most localities is $4,060 . But in Northern Virginia (Arlington, Fairfax, Loudoun and Prince William counties) it is $5,403. It is also $5,403 for certain cities such as Alexandria, Fairfax, Falls Church, Manassas and Manassas Park.

If the Applicant in the above example, lived in Fairfax County and decided to transfer $98,000 he would be disqualified for 18 months:

$$\$98,000/\$5,403 = 18.14 \text{ months}$$

VDSS rounds this value down to 18 months.

But if he lived in Lee County, where the average cost of nursing home care is currently $4,060 he would be disqualified for 24 months:

$$\$98,000/\$4,060 = 24.14 \text{ or } 24 \text{ months}$$

You might think that the period of ineligibility starts from the date of the transfer, but the *Transfer of Assets Rule* contained within Virginia Administrative Code (12 VAC 30-40-300) states:

> The period of ineligibility shall begin on the first day of the first month during or after which assets have been transferred for less than fair market value and which does not occur in any other period of ineligibility under this section.

What??

Does this mean that if I transfer assets on March 15th, my Penalty Period begins on March 1st — or does this mean that if I transfer assets on March 15th, my Penalty Period begins on April 1st???

The rule can be read both ways. And that is not the only unknown. The Penalty Period is computed when the person applies for Medicaid. The VDSS will divide the value of the transfer by the value of nursing care in the county (or city) at the time the Application is filed and not the value in effect when the transfer was made (12 VAC 30-40-300).

Luckily, the cost of nursing care continues to increase, so the Penalty Period might be significantly less than was figured by the Applicant at the time he made his transfer.

Bottom line. Before you transfer assets, it is best to consult with an Elder Law attorney who will tell you the current value of nursing care in your county, and how VDSS is interpreting this law.

If the Penalty Period is significant, you need to consult with the attorney again before you file the application to be sure that your projection of the Penalty Period is still valid.

The strategy of transferring all his assets and waiting a year or two may not be an option if our single Applicant needs immediate nursing care. In such case, the adage "half a loaf is better than none" applies; only in legal circles we refer to it as the **Rule of Halves**. The concept is simple. The Applicant gives away a certain amount of money to trigger a Penalty Period for a certain amount of time and yet keeping enough money for his care during the Penalty Period. For example, suppose our single Applicant who has $100,000 finds that he needs to use $4,000 of his savings each month to pay for his nursing care. If the average cost of nursing care as set by the VDSS in his county is $4,060 and the Applicant gives half of his savings to his child it will trigger a 12 month Penalty Period:

$$\$50,000 / \$4,060 = 12.31 \text{ months or one year}$$

During that Penalty Period the Applicant will use the remaining $50,000 to pay for his nursing care. If he needs to use $4,000 of his savings each month to pay for his nursing care, at the end of the year he should have $ 2,000 left. He is allowed $2,000 so he can apply for Medicaid. He will report the $50,000 transfer to VDSS, and they will note that the Penalty Period has passed. All other things equal, the Applicant should qualify for Medicaid at that time.

Of course, it may be that the Applicant may need to use more or less than $4,000 of his savings each month to pay for his care. The amount he gives away needs to be adjusted accordingly. Although the Rule of Halves is easy to understand, implementing it needs careful consideration. It is important to consult with an Elder Law attorney who can calculate the proper balance between gift and monies that need to be reserved for the Applicant's care during the Penalty Period.

JUST GIVE IT ALL AWAY

The strategy we have been discussing can be used if the Applicant needs nursing care in the near future. But it may happen that a person is diagnosed in the early stages of a progressive disease that is expected to ultimately result in a lengthy stay in a nursing facility. A person in such a situation may decide to give his property away, with the hope that he will not need long term nursing care for at least three years.

The three years is the **_Look-back period_** that VDSS uses to investigate the finances of a person who applies for Medicaid. The Look-back period increases to five years from the date of application for Medical Assistance if there was a transfer into a Trust (42 U.S.C. 1396p(c);VA 32.1-325.02). If VDSS determines that the Applicant, or his spouse, made transfers during the Look-back period, they will impose a Penalty Period equal to the sum total of all uncompensated transfers during the Look-back period divided by the average cost of nursing care in the county (or city) at the time the application is filed (12 VAC 30-4-300).

 THERE IS NO LIMIT ON THE PENALTY PERIOD

Although VDSS will look back only three years for trans-fers, there is no limit on the Penalty Period imposed for that transfer. For example, suppose the Applicant gives his child $300,000. If he applies for Medicaid within three years from the date of transfer, and the average cost of nursing care in his county is $4,060, he can be denied Medicaid benefits for more than six years.

$300,000/$4,060 = 73 months or 6.08 years

Of course the way to avoid the problem is to transfer the funds and not apply within the Look-back Period. But if the transfer was made into an irrevocable Trust, during the Look-back Period, the Applicant may be stuck with the full 73 months because, as discussed, if funds were transferred into a Trust, the state has the right to look back five years and impose the full penalty for the transfer.

And this is not a game of "Catch me if you can." Under both state and federal law, the Applicant and his spouse (or whoever applies for him) are required to make a full disclosure of transfers made during these periods. Anyone who knowingly and wilfully makes a false statement in an application for Medicaid can be convicted for Medicaid fraud. In addition to criminal penalties, whoever commits the fraud will be required to return all incorrect benefits to the state, plus one and one-half percent each month on the amount of benefits paid from the date payment was made for the Recipient (VA 32.1-321.3).

The reader may be thinking "Yes, but if I don't make a transfer into a Trust, all the law requires is that I report transfers made within the previous 3 years. If I come down with an illness that I know will cause me to deteriorate over a period of time, all I need do is give all my money to my child; be sure to wait three years and I will qualify for Medicaid. My child will keep my money safe. Should I need that money, my child will return as much as I need. Money that I don't use will be protected for my child."

The Medicaid Qualifying Plan of giving away all assets and then waiting three years is certainly allowed under the law, but this is a "brute force" approach to the problem. There's no finesse. It is a drastic step to take and fraught with peril.

Once the money is transferred, a completed gift is made. The child becomes the legal owner of the money and with all of the obvious "what ifs."

What if the child goes bankrupt or dies?

What if the child is sued? Will a Court order the child to use the money you gave to pay the judgment?

What if the child is divorced? Will the Court decide that your child's spouse is entitled to half of that money?

But the real problem is the loss of independence. Being impoverished at a time in your life when you are unable to supplement your income, and when your physical health is declining, can lead to much sadness. Imagine going to your child and asking for money. Imagine the child thinking, or worse yet, asking
                    "What's the money for?"

And what if you give the money away and never need nursing care? Medical technology is advancing with amazing speed. Although few cures have been found for mankind's ills, there have been many breakthroughs in their treatment. With modern drugs, many patients are now able to function without the need for long-term care. Even those who have been diagnosed with a progressive disease may not need nursing care for several years — maybe never.

Meanwhile, the money is gone, and your independence along with it.

Giving away all one's money and then waiting three years works, but at the cost of your independence. Putting money into an irrevocable Trust and waiting five years has its risks. A lot can happen in that time. You could require full nursing care the day after you transfer your assets into the Trust. Maybe the five year look-back is changed to a six year look back period.

For those in good health, an alternative is to do nothing until you actually need nursing home care and then implement a Medicaid qualifying strategy at that time. Of course, there is the chance that you take suddenly ill, say with a stroke, and are unable to implement a Medicaid Qualifying plan. A Durable Power Of Attorney that is properly drafted and signed while you have capacity should solve the problem. You can appoint someone to be your Attorney In Fact to implement a Medicaid Qualifying plan for you.

It is important that the Durable Power of Attorney be properly drafted. In December 2002, A New Jersey Court refused to allow a son to transfer property on behalf of his incapacitated mother for the purpose of qualifying for Medicaid. Although his mother gave him a Power of Attorney authorizing him to apply for Medicaid on her behalf, the Court refused to allow the transfer because the Power of Attorney "... did not provide for him to make gifts on her behalf to himself or anyone else, either to qualify her for Medicaid or for any other reason" (*In the Matter of Mildred Keri*, Superior Court of New Jersey, Appellate Division, A-5949-01T5). This case was reversed by the New Jersey Supreme Court and eventually the son was able to transfer the assets on behalf of his mother. But a transfer of property under an improperly drafted Power of Attorney can still be challenged.

The VDSS may challenge transfers made under a Power of Attorney that does not give the Attorney-In-Fact specific authority to implement a Medicaid Qualifying plan. It is important that your Power of Attorney be drafted by an Elder Law attorney who knows what provisions to include in the document so that it will stand up to VDSS scrutiny.

 THE ONLY THING CERTAIN IS CHANGE

The discussion relating to Medicaid Qualifying Plans for the Commonwealth of Virginia is not intended to lull the reader into a false sense of security. The only thing certain about federal and state laws is that they will change. Whatever strategy you choose may not be around when you need it.

There is a bill pending in the Virginia legislature (House Bill 2601, offered January 12, 2005) which if passed will give the Department of Medical Assistance Services the right to ask the federal government for a waiver of their rules relating to Medicaid. The legislature wants to make the rules regulating the transfer of assets much more restrictive. For example, they want to change the Look-Back Period to six years. As we will see in the next chapter, federal law allows the Applicant's home to be transferred to certain relatives. The legislature wants to prohibit such transfers. They also want to restrict transfers to a disabled child such that the assets are placed in a Trust for the sole benefit of the child, and upon the child's death whatever remains in the Trust goes to the state of Virginia to recover monies it spent for the child's care.

In addition to the proposed change in Virginia law, there is a proposal in the federal government to give the states autonomy in the administration of the Medicaid program for the elderly in need of nursing care.

If states are given autonomy in the administration of the long-term nursing care program, the changes proposed by the Virginia legislature could very well become law.

The point is that there is no certainty when it comes to future Medicaid qualifying options.

But we did not write this chapter to give the reader a definitive Medicaid Qualifying strategy. Rather, it was to give the reader an understanding of the law as it relates to qualifying for Medicaid; and to let the reader know that under current law, options are available should the need for long-term nursing care arise in the future.

We also wrote this chapter to let the general public understand how this federal program is administered here in the state of Virginia. And, incidentally, we touched only on the basics. There are other, more sophisticated, Medicaid Qualifying options available that an experienced Elder Law attorney can explain to you. The prudent thing to do is to visit an Elder Law attorney if and when you become concerned about a long term care problem. He can explain current law to you as it relates to qualifying for Medicaid. He can suggest the best path for you to follow, given your set of circumstances.

It is also important to keep up with changes in policy both in the state and federal government; and to let your legislators know how you feel about such changes. If you are in favor of (or against) House Bill 2601 contact the Board of Medical Assistance Services and voice your opinion.

Protecting the Homestead 11

We discussed the problem of having cash assets in excess of that allowed under current federal and state law; but what about the person whose only asset of value is his home? As explained in Chapter 10, whether the home counts as an asset for purposes of qualifying for Medicaid depends on whether his spouse or dependent family member is occupying the home. Even if no family member occupies the home, the Applicant cannot be denied Medicaid benefits because he owns a home, provided he says he intends to return to his home. However, once he receives Medicaid benefits, the state has the right to have a physician determine whether the Recipient can reasonably be expected to return home within a year. If not, the state has a right to place a lien on the property for monies spent on his behalf.

Even though the state does not place a lien on his home during his lifetime, if the Medicaid Recipient received Medical Assistance after age 55, the state can seek recovery from the sale of his home once the home is sold or he dies. The state will not seek recovery from a home owned by a deceased Recipient while his spouse, or minor or disabled child are living there. However, once the child reaches 21, or the spouse and disabled child are deceased, whoever inherits the home will need to pay off that lien or the state can force the sale of the property and take the money from the proceeds of the sale (42 U.S.C. 1396p).

In this chapter we discuss ways to protect the home from such a *Medicaid Lien*.

TRANSFERRING THE HOME

Protecting the homestead is easy to do if the Medicaid Recipient is married. Under state and federal law, the Applicant can transfer his home to the Community Spouse without penalty. He can make the transfer either before or after he applies for Medicaid (42 U.S.C. 1396p(c)2A).

If the home is in the name of the Medicaid Recipient only, he can sign a deed transferring the property to his spouse. If he and the Community Spouse own the property jointly, they can sign a deed transferring the property to the Community Spouse. It is important to make the transfer of the joint interest because the property would be in the Applicant's name only in the event the Community Spouse died first. In such case, the property would be available to reimburse the state for monies spent.

Protecting the homestead is more of a problem for the aged, single parent; and it is a problem for aging parents who both are not in the best of health. Who knows which of them will require long term nursing care? Maybe both will need such care. Maybe neither of them will require nursing care.

Most parents want to have their children inherit the one thing the parent has of value, namely their home. Parents fear that if they ever need Medicaid benefits, their home will be sold to reimburse the state. This idea is so distressing to some parents that even though they are in relatively good health, they may decide to transfer their home to their child with the understanding that the parents will continue to live there for the rest of their lives. Those planning such a move need to understand that they are trading one risk (need to apply for Medicaid) for several other risks.

⊠ RISK OF LOSS

Once you transfer the property to your child it becomes his property and that property can be lost or used to pay for his debts just like anything else he owns. Your child could run into serious financial difficulties. Your child could be sued. This is especially a risk if your child is a professional (doctor, nurse, accountant, financial planner, attorney, etc.). If your child is found to be personally liable for damages, your home could become part of the settlement of that law suit.

If your child is (or gets) married, this complicates matters even more so. If the child divorces, the value of your home might be included as part of the property settlement agreement. This may be to your child's detriment because the child may need to share the value of the property with his former spouse. If you do not transfer the property, it cannot become part of his marital equation.

Even if your child is single there is a risk of loss. Your child may want to take out a business loan. If the loan is significant, the lender will want to include everything your child owns as collateral (security for the debt). If the lender learns that you are occupying the house, he will especially want to include your house as collateral because that will motivate your son to repay the loan.

The point is, transferring the house to your child could be bad for both of you. And that is not the only downside.

⊠   POSSIBLE GIFT TAX

A Gift Tax needs to be paid if the value of the equity in your home (plus the value of all the gifts you gave over your lifetime in excess of the Annual Gift Tax Exclusion) exceeds the lifetime Gift Tax Exclusion. The current lifetime Gift Tax Exclusion is $1,000,000, so for most of us, this is not a problem. Yet there still is the hassle of filing a Gift Tax return.

⊠   POSSIBLE CAPITAL GAINS TAX

Although Congress has expressed its intent to phase out the Estate Tax, there is no discussion to do away with the Capital Gains Tax. If you gift the property to the child during your lifetime, when he sells the property he will pay a Capital Gains Tax on the increase in value from the price you paid for your home to the selling price at the time your child sells the property.

If you do not make the gift during your lifetime, the child will inherit the property with a step-up in basis, i.e., he will inherit the property at its market value as of the date of your death. Under today's tax structure and continuing until 2009, that step-up in basis is unlimited. If your child sells the property when he inherits it, he will pay no Capital Gains Tax, regardless of how large the step-up in basis.

In 2010, there will be a limit on the amount that can be inherited free of the Capital Gains Tax but that limit is quite high so for most of us this is not a concern.

⊠ POSSIBLE LOSS OF GOVERNMENT BENEFITS

If you are married and you transfer property to someone other than your spouse, then depending upon the value of the transfer, both you and your spouse could be disqualified from receiving Medicaid or Supplemental Security Income ("SSI") if you apply within three years from the date of transfer of the property. That increases to five years if you transfer the property into a Trust. It could happen that during that period of time, one of you takes suddenly ill and requires long-term nursing care.

Why jeopardize your right to receive Medicaid for both of you? Owning a homestead will not disqualify you from receiving Medicaid, but transferring it may make you and your spouse ineligible for a long time.

The elderly parent, who is single, may not be convinced that gifting the house is a bad idea. He may be thinking "By giving my home to my child, I risk not being able to qualify for Medicaid for three years. If I don't make the gift and need Medicaid at any time during the rest of my lifetime, the state will get the house for sure."

But there are better Estate Plans than the outright gift. The Life Estate strategy may be one of them.

You can give the property to your child, and keep a Life Estate for yourself. Your child will have no right to your homestead while you are alive so you have no fear that the property can be lost or taken from you during your lifetime. Upon your death, your child will own the property 100%, and without the need for Probate.

Depending on the value of your home, this Life Estate approach might allow you to shorten the Medicaid transfer Penalty Period, because you are not giving your child the full value of your home, you are just giving away the value of the Remainder Interest i.e., what is left of the property after your death.

The value of the Remainder Interest depends on your life expectancy. A gift of a Remainder Interest when you are 90 is worth more to your child than when you are 50.

DETERMINING THE VALUE OF THE REMAINDER INTEREST

The Centers for Medicare and Medicaid Services publishes a table of values for the Life Estate Interest and the Remainder Interest based on the age of the Grantor at the time of the transfer (State Medicaid Manual, Part 3 (SM3 3258.9) LIFE ESTATE AND REMAINDER INTEREST TABLE). You can find excerpts from this table, at the Public Information section of the Eagle Publishing Company Web site.   http://www.eaglepublishing.com

Fortunately, this table goes up to age 109, so the value they assign to the Remainder Interest is relatively low. For example, according to this table, if a 70 year old makes a transfer to his son and keeps a Life Estate for himself, his Life Estate is equal to 61% of the value of the property. The Remainder Interest is worth only 39%.

The actual percentage given in the table for the Remainder Interest is .39478. If the father's equity in the home** is $100,000 it means the value of the gift of the Remainder Interest is $39,478.

** fair market value less monies owed on the property

This greatly reduces the Penalty Period. If he transferred the house and did not keep a Life Estate, his penalty period in a county whose average nursing care is $4,060 would be two years:

$100,000/$4,060 = 24 months or 2 years

By keeping a Life Estate the Penalty Period reduces to nine months: $39,478/$4,060 = 9.72 or 9 months.

If you live in a county with average nursing care of $4,684 the results are equally impressive:

$100,000/$5,403 = 18.51 or 18 months
$39,478/$5,403 = 7.31 or 7 months

 THE LIFE ESTATE IS NOT
A COMPLETE SOLUTION

A Life Estate is a better Medicaid Qualifying Plan than an outright gift but only for purposes of shortening the period of ineligibility. Issues of control and taxes and recovery still remain.

CONTROL

You will not be able to sell your home, or get a mortgage on the property, without permission from your child.

TAX ISSUES

And, as explained at the end of Chapter 2, if you sell the home, you might need to pay a Capital Gains tax.

RECOVERY BY THE STATE

Under Federal law, the state has the right to recover monies spent on your behalf if you received nursing care under Medicaid after the age of 55. Monies can be recovered from property you owned at the time of your death. This includes property you own jointly with another, and property in which you own a Life Estate interest (42 U.S.C. 1396p(b)(4)(B)).

As of this writing, the state of Virginia has not sought recovery from property in which the Medicaid Recipient owned a Life Estate interest. But the law is on the books and state policy could change in the future.

Before you decide to transfer your home to your child and keep a Life Estate for yourself, it is important to check with an Elder Law attorney to investigate the full consequences of the transfer.

TRANSFERS THAT PROTECT

As explained, you can own a home and still qualify for Medicaid, but there still is the concern that once you become a Medicaid recipient, the state may place a Medicaid Lien on your homestead for monies spent on your behalf. Under current law, there are several ways to protect your home from such lien. For a married person, the home can be protected by transferring it to the Community Spouse.

TRANSFERRING THE HOME TO THE SPOUSE

The Applicant is free to transfer his home to his spouse either before or after he qualifies for Medicaid. Once the house is in the name of the Community Spouse, she can arrange to have it inherited by a family member and not the Medicaid Recipient. Should the Applicant be too ill to make the transfer himself, the deed can be signed by his Attorney-In-Fact under a properly drafted Durable Power of Attorney. If he did not give such authority, and he is too ill to sign his name, it may be necessary to have a Conservator appointed who can ask the Court for permission to make the transfer.

Establishing a conservatorship may be expensive and time consuming, but it is important that the homestead be transferred to the Community Spouse because it could happen that the Community Spouse dies first leaving the home in the name of the now single Medicaid recipient. The downside is that there is no guarantee that the judge will allow the transfer of the homestead to the Community Spouse. Before you apply for a conservatorship it is important to ask your attorney whether such transfers have been allowed in the past.

Under state and federal law, if an Applicant owns his home together with a sibling and the sibling lived with the Applicant for at least one year before entering the nursing facility, the Applicant can transfer the home to the sibling without a Medicaid transfer penalty (42 U.S.C. 1396p). This law presents an opportunity for an unmarried Applicant who has a brother or sister to protect the homestead. The only question is how the sibling becomes co-owner. If the Applicant and his sibling purchased the property together, and the sibling lived in the home for a year prior to the Applicant entering the nursing home, then the sibling's interest in the property is protected. The Applicant can transfer his share of the homestead to his sibling without penalty, and that will protect all of the homestead.

If the house is in the Applicant's name only, then it is important to consult with an Elder Law attorney to determine the best way for the sibling to become part owner of the home. Federal law only requires that the sibling have an *equity interest* in the property. An equity interest could be joint ownership or a Tenancy-In-Common or a Remainder Interest in the homestead. An Elder Law attorney will be able to suggest a method of transferring an equity interest to the sibling that will result in a Penalty Period of a year or less. The attorney will also assist with preparing documentation to present to VDSS to verify that:

⇨ the sibling owns an equity interest in the home

⇨ the Penalty Period for the transfer has passed

⇨ the sibling occupied the home for a year prior to the Applicant entering the nursing home.

TRANSFER TO A CAREGIVER CHILD

A similar law applies to the Medicaid recipient who owns his home and wants to transfer it to his child. The federal law allows a transfer of the homestead to the child without penalty, provided the child lived with and took care of his parent for at least two years before the parent entered the nursing home.

There is no requirement that the child own an equity interest in the property; but the federal statute does require that the state verify that the child lived in the home and provided care to the parent for the two years; and that this care enabled the parent to remain at home rather than be placed in a nursing home (42 U.S.C. 1396p(c)(2)(A)(iv)).

If the value of the house is not greater than the two year Penalty Period it may be just as easy to transfer the home to the child and wait out the two years. Specifically, if the Applicant lives in a county where the average cost of nursing care is $4,060, a transfer of $97,440 will result in a two year penalty period: $4,060 x 24 = $97,440.

If the parent's equity in the home is worth no more than $97,440, the home can be transferred to the child without the need for the child to prove to VDSS that care was given to the parent over that two year period.

If the home is worth significantly more, it is important to consult with an Elder Law attorney, preferably prior to the two year period. The attorney will explain how to document that care over the two year period so that the information can be presented to the VDSS when the parent applies for Medical Assistance.

Some of the things the VDSS will want to know are:

⇨ the Applicant's medical condition during the two year period

⇨ whether the child lived in the home for the required time period

⇨ what care was provided by the child that enabled the parent to remain at home rather than being placed in an institution

⇨ how many hours per day were spent by the child in caring for his parent

⇨ Whether the child worked outside of the home during the two year period; and if so, who cared for the parent while the child was at work.

The VDSS may want a friend or family member to verify that the child did provide the necessary care during the two years.

Once it is established by VDSS that federal requirements are satisfied, the property can be transferred to the child without affecting the right of the Applicant to receive Medicaid benefits (12 VAC 30-40-300).

TRANSFERRING THE HOME TO A DISABLED CHILD

In Virginia, the Applicant or his spouse may transfer their home or any other of their Resources to a child (minor or adult) who is blind, or disabled without penalty (42 U.S.C. 1396p(c)(2A). In the event that the child does not have a determination of blindness or disability from the Social Security Administration, the VDSS will need to review the child's medical records to determine whether the child meets the criteria (12 VAC 30-40-300).

If the child is receiving Social Security disability benefits, the parent can transfer their home or other assets to a Special Needs Trust for the child (see Chapter 7). This transfer will not disqualify the child (or the parent) from receiving government benefits, provided the Trust is drafted according to state and federal law.

 DON'T TRY THIS ON YOUR OWN

A Medicaid Qualifying Plan is not something to attempt on your own. The Medicaid program is complex and volatile. There are many levels of law that govern Medicaid. There are the federal statutes (Social Security Act Title XIX/P.L. 89-97); the U.S. Code of Federal Regulations (42 CFR 430-435) and the Centers for Medicare and Medicaid Services State Medicaid Manual, Part 3 that say how the federal statutes are to be administered in the United States.

There are the Virginia Medicaid statutes (Code of Virginia, Section 32.1-32 through 32.1-332); and Chapter 12 of the Virginia Administrative Code that explains how the Medicaid program is to be administered in the Commonwealth of Virginia.

These five different sets of laws and regulations are constantly changing — often with little or no notice to the general public.

And the laws are not well written.

In *Rehabilitation Association of Virginia v. Kozlowski*, 42 F.3d 1444, 1450 (4th Cir 1994), the Court had nothing but sympathy for officials who must interpret or administer these laws. "There can be no doubting that the statutes and provisions in question, involving the financing of Medicare and Medicaid, are among the most completely impenetrable texts within human experience. Indeed, one approaches them . . . with dread, for not only are they dense reading of the most tortuous kind, but Congress also revisits the area frequently, generously cutting and pruning in the process and making any solid grasp of the matters addressed merely a passing phase."

Judges in the federal District Court were equally critical: "The Social Security Act is among the most intricate ever drafted by Congress. Its Byzantine construction ... makes the Act 'almost unintelligible to the uninitiated.' ... The District Court ... described the Medicaid statute as 'an aggravated assault on the English language, resistant to attempts to understand it'." (*Schweiker v. Gray Panthers*, 453 U.S. 34(1981)).

Most states have a manual that they provide to workers who are in charge of implementing the Medicaid Program. In Virginia, the MEDICAID MANUAL explains how eligibility is to be determined when an Applicant applies. Even with a Manual, the program is not uniformly administered because of the complexity of the law. Many of the state laws are not spelled out clearly, as was the case with the example of the period of ineligibility given in the previous chapter.

Many of the laws and regulations have not been challenged in court, so as yet no Judge has explained how the law should be applied in the state of Virginia. This is the case with Medicaid Annuities. The Virginia Department of Social Services issued an an administrative ruling in their Medicad Eligibility Manual Volume XIII M1140.260 stating that as of December 1, 2004, an Annuity would not qualify as an Exempt Resource unless the Commonwealth of Virginia was named as the beneficiary in the event the Annuitant died.

There is no statute on either on the state or federal level requiring the state to be beneficiary, yet if you purchase an Annuity and do not name the state as beneficiary, the VDSS office in your county can consider the purchase as an impermissible transfer of funds. Should they do so, you will have no choice but to appeal their ruling. As we will see, unless you are trying to prove a point, the appeal is not the way to go.

THE MEDICAID APPEAL

An Applicant who is denied Medicaid Assistance benefits can appeal the ruling by mailing a *Request For Appeal* to the Division of Client Appeals. He can get the address from the VDSS. The Applicant must file his request within thirty days of his receipt of the VDSS notice that the Applicant has been denied benefits. If he is too ill to do so, a family member, or other person acting on his behalf, may do so for him (12 VAC 30-110-10, 30-110-60, 30-110-130, 30-110-140, 30-110-160).

Once the Request For Appeal is received the Department of Medical Assistance Services will appoint a Hearing Officer to review the facts of the case and conduct an informal hearing on the matter (12 VAC 30-110-220, 30-110-310). Even though the Hearing is an informal proceeding, it is, none-the-less, a complex legal process. To win you will need have a complete understanding of all applicable law. You will need to know how to discover and present evidence to prove your case. It is important that you have an attorney present at the hearing to represent the Applicant. If he cannot afford to employ an attorney, ask Legal Services for assistance. See Page xiii for the Legal Services office nearest you.

After conducting the hearing, the Hearing Officer will send a written final decision (12 VAC 30-110-370). More likely than not, he will rule against the Applicant. After all, he is asking an officer of the Department of Medical Assistance Services to rule that the VDSS applied the administrative code incorrectly. The Hearing Officer is not likely to come to that conclusion.

The next step in the appeals process is to bring the case before a Judge of the Virginia Circuit Court. The Judge will take a broader look at the picture and consider state and federal law, as well as Constitutional rights under the law. If the Applicant is turned down in the state Court, he can appeal to a federal court — all the way up to the United States Supreme Court.

The appeal process is expensive, stressful and time consuming. It is important to employ an attorney to help with the appeal and that can be expensive. In Chapter 10 we presented many different options that are legally available to the Applicant at this time. The goal is to get him qualified for Medicaid as quickly as possible, and with the least amount of hassle. It is better to choose a strategy that has been allowed in the past, rather than chance a denial of the application and be forced to appeal the decision.

An experienced Elder Law attorney can explain what strategies have been allowed in the past in your county and which strategies are likely to be challenged. The key word is "experienced." Before employing an attorney, determine what percentage of his practice is devoted to Medicaid eligibility; how long he has practiced Elder Law in that county; and whether he is familiar with the appeals process, should the need arise.

Guiding Those You Love 12

Once you are satisfied with your Estate Plan, the final thing to consider is whether your heirs will be able to locate your assets after you're gone.

Most people have their business records in one place, their Will in another place, car titles and deeds in still another place. When someone dies, their beneficiaries may feel as if they are playing a game of "hide and seek" with the decedent. The game might be fun were it not for the fact that unlocated items may be forever lost. For example, suppose you die in an accident and no one knows you are insured by your credit card company for accidental death in the amount of $25,000. The only one to profit is the insurance company, which is just that much richer because no one told them that you died as a result of an accident.

And how about a key to a safe deposit box? Will anyone find it? Even if they find the key, how will they locate the box?

It is not difficult to arrange things so that your affairs are always in order. It amounts to being aware of what you own (and owe) and keeping a record of your possessions. A side benefit is that by doing so, you will always know where all your business records are. If you ever spent time trying to collect information to file your taxes or trying to find a lost stock or bond certificate, you will appreciate the value of organizing your records.

POINTING THE WAY

Heirs need all the help they can get. It is difficult enough dealing with the loss, without the frustration of trying to locate important documents. Your heirs will have no problem locating your assets if you keep all of your records in a single place. It can be a desk drawer or a file cabinet or even a shoe box. It is helpful if you keep a separate file or folder for each type of investment. You might consider setting up the following folders:

📁 THE BANK & SECURITIES FOLDER

Store your original certificates for stocks, bonds, mutual funds, certificates of deposit, in a folder labeled **BANK & SECURITIES FOLDER.** In addition to the original certificate include a copy of the contract you signed with each financial institution. The contract will show where you have funds and who you named as beneficiary or joint owner of the account. If someone owes you money and has signed a promissory note or mortgage that identifies you as the lender, then you can store these documents in this folder as well.

If you wish to store your original documents in a safe deposit box, then keep a record of the location of the safe deposit box, and the number of the box, in this folder. Make a copy of all of the items stored in the box and place the copies in this folder. If you have an extra key to the box, then put it in the folder. If you are the only person with access to the box, it may take a Probate proceeding to remove items from the box once you die. Consider giving someone you trust the right to gain entry to the box in the event of your incapacity or death.

📁 THE INSURANCE FOLDER

The INSURANCE FOLDER is for each insurance policy that you own, be it life insurance, car insurance, homeowner's insurance or a health care insurance. If you purchased real property, you may have received a title commitment at closing and the original title insurance policy some weeks later when you received your original deed from recording. If you cannot locate the title insurance policy, contact the closing agent and have them send you a copy of your title insurance policy.

📁 THE PENSION AND ANNUITY FOLDER

Put all of the documents relating to your pension or annuity in this folder. Include the telephone number and/or address of the person to contact in the event of your death.

FOR FEDERAL RETIREES

If you are a Federal Retiree, you should have received your **PERSONAL IDENTIFICATION NUMBER (PIN)** and the person who will inherit your pension (your *survivor annuitant*) should have received his/her own PIN as well. It is relatively simple to obtain this during your lifetime, but it may be difficult and/or stressful for your survivor annuitant to work through the system once you are gone.

Survivor annuitant benefits are not automatic. Your survivor annuitant must apply for them by submitting a death claim to the Office of Personnel Management. Your survivor needs to know that it is necessary to apply and also how to apply. You can call the Office of Personnel Management at (888) 767-6738 to get printed information that you can keep in this folder to guide your survivor annuitant through the process. You can also download information from their Web site: http://www.opm.gov

🗁 THE DEED FOLDER

Many people save every scrap of paper associated with the closing of real property. If you closed recently on real estate and there was a mortgage involved in the purchase, you probably walked away from closing with enough paper to wallpaper your kitchen. If you wish, you can keep all of those papers in a separate file that identifies the property, for example:

CLOSING PAPERS FOR THE ARLINGTON PROPERTY

Place the original deed (or a copy if the original is in a safe deposit box) in a separate **DEED FOLDER**. Include cemetery deeds, condominium deeds, timesharing certificates, deed to out of state property, etc. Also include a copy of related documents such as an Abstract of Title, or a recorded condominium approval. If you have a title insurance policy, put the original in the insurance folder, and a copy in this folder. If you have a mortgage on your property, put a copy of the recorded mortgage and promissory note in a separate **LIABILITY FOLDER**. Once the mortgage is paid off, the lender should give you Satisfaction of Mortgage. The Satisfaction needs to be recorded. You can keep the recorded Satisfaction together with the deed to the property.

LOCATING REAL PROPERTY

If you own a vacant lot, your beneficiaries will find the deed (or a copy) in this folder but that deed will not contain the address of that property because it doesn't have one. The post office does not assign a street address until there is a building on the site. Your beneficiary could get the location of the property from city or county records. But why make things hard for them? Include a simple handwritten note in this folder that tells them exactly how to locate the property.

🗁 THE TAX RECORD FOLDER

Your Personal Representative (or next of kin) will need to file your final income tax returns. Keep a copy of your tax returns (both federal and state) for the past three years in your Tax Record Folder. As explained in Chapter 3, beginning in 2010, there will be a cap on the step-up basis to 4.3 million dollars for property inherited by your spouse and 1.3 million for property inherited by anyone else. It is important to keep a record of the basis of your property, not only for your heirs, but for yourself should you decide to sell the property during your lifetime. If you purchase real property, you need to keep a record of the purchase price as well as monies you paid to improve the property. You need these records to determine whether a Capital Gains Tax is due on the transfer. Your accountant can help you set up a bookkeeping system to keep a running record of your basis in everything you own of value.

🗁 THE LIABILITY FOLDER

The LIABILITY FOLDER should contain all loan documents of debts that you owe. For example, if you purchased real property and have a mortgage on that property, put a copy of the mortgage and promissory note in this folder. If you owe money on a car, put the loan documents here. A lease is a liability, because you have contracted to pay a certain amount for the period of the lease, so include a copy of any lease agreement in this Liability Folder. If you have a credit card, put a copy of the contract you signed with the credit card company in this folder.

Many people never take the time to calculate their net worth (what a person owns less what that person owes). By having a record of your assets and outstanding debts, you can calculate your net worth whenever you wish.

🗂 THE PERSONAL PROPERTY FOLDER

MOTOR VEHICLES

Put all motor vehicle titles in a Personal Property Folder. This includes cars, mobile homes, boats, planes, etc. If you owe money on the vehicle, the lender may have possession of the title certificate. If such is the case, put a copy of the title certificate and registration in this folder and a copy of the loan documents in a separate liability folder. If you own a boat or plane, identify the location of the motor vehicle. For example, if you are leasing space in an airplane hangar or in a marina, keep a copy of the leasing agreement in this folder.

JEWELRY

If you own expensive jewelry, keep a picture of the item together with the sales receipt or written appraisal in this folder.

COLLECTOR'S ITEMS

If you own a valuable art or coin collection, or any other item of significant value, include a picture of the item in this folder. Also include evidence of ownership of the item, such as a sales receipt or a certificate of authenticity, or a written appraisal of the property.

🗂 THE PERSONAL RECORDS FOLDER

The **PERSONAL RECORDS FOLDER** should include documents that relate to you personally, such as a birth certificate, naturalization papers, marriage certificate, divorce papers, military records, social security card; etc.

📁 THE ESTATE PLANNING DOCUMENT FOLDER

WILL/TRUST

Place your Will and/or Trust in a separate folder. If the original document is in a safe deposit box, then place a copy of the document in this folder together with instructions about how to find the original. If you placed your Will with the Probate Court, put the address of the Court in the folder together with a copy of the Will.

It is important to keep a copy of your Will or Trust because over the years you may forget what provision you made. Keeping a copy in your home may save you the time and effort to retrieve the document, just to determine whether it needs to be updated.

PRENUPTIAL/POSTNUPTIAL AGREEMENT

Prenuptial or postnuptial agreements usually provide for the disposition of your property upon your death, so a copy of the agreement should be included in this folder.

OTHER ESTATE PLANNING DOCUMENTS

You can include the original or a copy of other Estate Planning Documents in this folder such as your:

⇨ Durable Power of Attorney,
⇨ Advance Medical Directive
⇨ Living Will
⇨ Prepaid Funeral Benefits Contract.

THE QUICK-FIND FOLDER

Many do not have the time, nor inclination, to "play" with all these folders. They do not anticipate an immediate demise. Getting hit by a truck, or dying in a fiery plane crash is not something to think about, much less prepare for. But consider that death is not the only problem. You could take suddenly ill (say with a stroke) and become incapacitated. Even the most time-starved optimist should have a murmur of concern that his loved ones will be left with a mess should something unforeseen happen.

If you do not feel like doing a complete job of organizing your records at this time, consider an abridged version. You can set up a single folder and place all of your important papers in that folder. You need to make the folder easily accessible to whoever you wish to manage your affairs in the event of your incapacity or death. You can do this by letting that person know of the existence of the folder and how to get it in an emergency.

You can keep the folder in an easily accessed place in your home with the folder identified as containing important papers. We labeled it "THE QUICK-FIND FOLDER" because the folder gives you and your family easy access to important information and/or documents. But you can create your own heading such as: "MY IMPORTANT PAPERS" or if you want a particular person to access the folder, you might label it: "RECORDS FOR MY SON, ROBERT"

It is helpful if you include a list of all you own and the location of each item in that folder.

We discussed people's natural disinclination to make an Estate Plan until they are faced with their own mortality. Many believe that they will make just one Will and then die (maybe that's why they put off making a Will). The reality is, most people who make a Will, change it at least once before they die. If you have an Estate Plan, it is important to update it when any of the following events take place:

✎ CHANGE IN MARITAL STATUS

There are two types of divorce that can be obtained in Virginia. A *Divorce from Bond of Matrimony* is a complete and final separation of the person and property of the couple. After the divorce all property (both real property and personal property) held by the couple as a Tenancy by the Entirety becomes a Tenancy In Common (VA 20-111). A *Divorce from Bed and Board* is much like a legal separation. The couple are separated, but neither can remarry.

If you obtain a Divorce from the Bond of Matrimony, unless your Final Judgment states otherwise, your former spouse has no right of survivorship in your property. If you die before you get around to changing your Will, any gift that you made in your Will or Trust to your former spouse is revoked. Your Probate Estate will be distributed as if your spouse died before you did (VA 64.1-59). This is not necessarily the case if you obtain a Divorce from Bed and Board (VA 20-95, 20-116).

Whichever type of Divorce you get, it is best not to just rely on the law. You need to review all of your Estate Planning documents (deeds, pension plans, insurance policies, Will or Trust etc.) and name a new beneficiary of your property.

NOTIFY EMPLOYER OF CHANGE

If you change your marital status (either marry or divorce) you need to tell your employer of the change so that the employer can change your status for purposes of paycheck tax deductions. If you have a health insurance plan or a pension plan, that provides benefits to your spouse, then these need to be changed as well.

✍ A CHANGE IN RELATIONSHIP

Getting married, separated or divorced; having a child; having a beneficiary of your Estate die, are all profound changes in one's life. When the dust settles, it is important to examine your Estate Plan to see if it needs revision. If you have a Trust, you can change it by having your attorney prepare an *amendment* to the Trust. If you have a Will, your attorney can prepare a *codicil* (a supplement) to the Will.

It is important to have changes made by a properly drafted and signed document. If you make changes by crossing things out or writing over your Will, or Trust, the validity of the document can be challenged once you die.

If you simply rip up the old Will, that will effectively revoke the Will (VA 64.1-58.1). But it could happen that someone (perhaps your attorney) has a copy of the Will. If no one knows that you revoked the Will, they may think the Will is lost and then offer the copy of the Will for Probate. If you draft a new Will, the first paragraph should say, "I revoke all prior Wills ..." This makes it clear that you want the new Will to replace all other Wills.

CAUTION

NEW SPOUSE OR CHILD CAN CHALLENGE OLD WILL

CHALLENGE BY SURVIVING SPOUSE

If you marry and "forget" to change the Will you prepared prior to your marriage, your spouse can challenge your Will unless:

⇨ the Will indicates that it is to be effective even after your marriage - or -

⇨ you and your spouse have a Marital Property Agreement that either provides for your spouse, or specifies that your spouse has no rights to your Estate.

If your spouse successfully challenges the Will prepared before the marriage, he/she is entitled to receive as much as she would have received if you died without a Will (VA 64.1-69.1)

CHALLENGE BY AFTERBORN CHILD

Children who are living at the time you sign your Will may be disinherited by just failing to mention them in your Will. If a child is born or adopted after you make your Will, unless you made provision for the *afterborn* outside of the Will, he is entitled to inherit as much as if you had died without a Will. If you made a gift in your Will to a child who was alive at the time, the afterborn is entitled to the <u>lesser</u> value of

⇨ the largest gift given to a child under your Will

⇨ the amount the afterborn would have received
    had you died without a Will (VA 64.1-70, 64.1-71).

The Court will decide how much of their inheritance your beneficiaries must contribute to make up the afterborn child's gift.

The laws relating to an afterborn child are complex and could lead to disagreement and hard feelings for those forced to contribute to the child's share. It is better to change your Will when a child is born so that your child receives no more, and no less, than you intended.

✍ BENEFICIARY MOVES OR DIES

Most people remember to name an alternate beneficiary should one of their beneficiaries die. But how many of us remember to notify the pension plan or insurance company when a beneficiary moves?

It is important that your beneficiary's address be available to those in charge of distributing funds upon your death. Many life insurance proceeds are never paid because the company cannot locate the beneficiary. The Actuarial Office of the Federal Employees' Group Life Insurance Program reported that as of September, 2003, they had over 55.8 million dollars in unpaid benefits, mostly because they could not locate the beneficiary at the last given address.

✍ RELOCATION TO A NEW STATE OR COUNTRY

There is no need to change your Estate Plan for a move within the state of Virginia. If you are moving to a different county in Virginia and you deposited your Will with the Clerk of the Court, you need to retrieve your Will and take it with you. Not all counties accept a Will for storage, so you need to check with the Clerk in the new county to determine if filing the Will with the Clerk is an option (VA 64.1-56).

If you are moving out of state and your attorney has your original Will or the original of any of your other Estate Planning documents, you need to retrieve these items to take with you to the new state.

You need to determine whether your Will conforms to the laws of the state of your new residence. Most states will honor a Will drafted according to Virginia law, however, the rights of a spouse vary considerably state to state. If you are married and have not provided the minimum amount as required by the laws of the new state, should you die before your spouse, your Will may be challenged on that basis. The same applies to a Trust. Many states allow a surviving spouse to demand funds from the Trust of the decedent spouse, if the deceased spouse did not provide the minimum amount to his spouse as required by the laws of that state.

LAWS OF DESCENT

If you do not have a Will, then it is important to check out the Laws of Descent for that state. In some states they are referred to as the *Laws of Intestate Succession*. Each state has its own laws relating to the inheritance of property and those laws are very different from each other. Who has the right to inherit your property in the Commonwealth of Virginia may be different from who can inherit your property in another state.

If you do not have a Will, then this is the time to think about who will inherit your property in the state of your new residence. This is important for those who are married. The right of a spouse to inherit property varies significantly from state to state. There is a world of difference in the rights of a spouse in a Community Property state (Arizona, California, Idaho, Louisiana, Nevada, New Mexico, Texas, Washington and Wisconsin) and other states. There is even variation in the rights of a spouse from one Community Property state to another!

A Will is Not Enough in Virginia

TAX CONSIDERATIONS

You need to check out the taxes of the new state. Each state has its own tax structure. Some states have an inheritance tax, or a transfer tax on all inherited property. If state taxes are high, you may need an Estate Plan that will minimize the impact of those taxes.

CREDITOR PROTECTION

Creditor protection is another item that is significantly different state to state. If you have much debt, then determine what items can be inherited by your family free of your debts in that state.

OTHER ESTATE PLANNING DOCUMENTS

Many states have laws directing physicians to honor a Medical Directive that is properly drafted in another state. Other states will not recognize a Medical Directive unless it is drafted according to the laws of that state. But even if the laws of the state honor your Virginia Advance Medical Directive, consider drafting another in the new state. Medical Directives vary significantly state to state. Other states may have laws that enable you to appoint someone with powers similar to a Health Care Agent, but the laws of the state may refer to such person as a *Patient Advocate* or a *Health Care Surrogate* or a *Health Care Representative.*

It is best to sign a new Health Care Directive using the form and terminology recognized in the new state, rather than chance any confusion should you become ill and find yourself in an emergency situation. Similarly, if you have appointed someone to handle your finances under a Power of Attorney, you may want to have another prepared in conformity with the laws of the new state, so there will be no question of the right of your Attorney-In-Fact to conduct business on your behalf.

RELOCATING THE MEDICAID RECIPIENT

If your family member is a Medicaid Recipient, and you want to move him to another state, you need to check out whether he will continue to be eligible for Medicaid in that state. As explained in Chapter 10, Medicaid is both a state and federal program. Once a person qualifies for Medicaid in one state, he can be transferred to another state; provided he qualifies under that state's Medical Assistance Program.

For example, Virginia does not have an upper limit for income, provided the Applicant's medical expenses are greater than the level of his non-exempt income. Other states have an *income cap*. Applicants whose income exceed that limit can be refused Medicaid benefits. If you plan to move a Medicaid Recipient to another state, it is important to first check with an Elder Law attorney in that state. He can explain the laws relating to Medicaid eligibility. As in Virginia, there are Medicaid qualifying techniques available under the laws of the state. For example, if the state has an income cap and your family member's income exceeds that value, an Elder Law attorney will be able to tell you what can be done in order to have the Recipient qualify for Medicaid in that state.

As you can see, state law has an important impact on your Estate Plan. When moving to another state, you need to educate yourself about the laws of that state, or consult with an attorney who can assist you in reviewing your Estate Plan to see if that plan will accomplish your goals in that state.

✍ A SIGNIFICANT CHANGE IN THE LAW

We pay our legislators (state and federal) to make laws and, if necessary, change those in effect. We pay judges to interpret the law and that interpretation may change the way the law operates. The legislature and the judiciary do their job and so laws change frequently. Tax laws are particularly volatile. The 2001 change in the Federal Estate Tax law gradually increases the Exclusion amount so that by 2010 no Federal Estate Tax will be due regardless of the value of your Estate. You may be thinking that there is no need for an Estate Tax plan because you don't intend to die prior to 2010. But any certainty relating to death and taxes is false security (especially taxes, in this case). As explained in Chapter 2, the law as passed in 2001, is effective only until December 31, 2010. If lawmakers do nothing, then on January 1, 2011, the Federal Estate Tax goes back into effect; and Estates that exceed one million dollars will once again be subject to Estate taxes.

And that is not the only uncertainty. Each state has its own Estate Tax structure. It remains to be seen how each state will react to the federal change. Some states may follow the lead of the federal government and increase their Estate Tax Exclusion in the same manner. Other states may see this as an opportunity to "pick up the slack" i.e., to increase their Estate Taxes, so that monies that would have been paid to the federal government will now be paid to the state.

You need to keep up with the news to learn about changes in the law that affect your Estate Plan. It is a good idea to check with your attorney on a regular basis to see if any change in the state or federal law affects your current Estate plan. And also check out the Eagle Publishing Company Web site for changes we will post to keep this book fresh.   http://www.eaglepublishing.com

Used to be, that housewives did a once a year, floor to ceiling, "spring housecleaning." We know of no survey telling whether today's houseperson conducts an annual purge of dirt and clutter. We suspect it went by the wayside when housewives entered the work force as full time employees. But it was a good practice. In many cases, it was the only time of the year when the house was truly clean and tidy. It is a good idea to incorporate that old-fashioned housecleaning practice to your financial records and clean them up on a regular basis. There is no need to keep the deed to real property that you have long since sold; a lease agreement to an apartment you no longer rent; a credit card to a closed account, etc.

Many hesitate to toss out some scrap of paper for fear it will not be available for future reference. There are documents you may need to keep for a lengthy period of time to establish a basis for tax purposes. You can avoid the problem of keeping too much, or not enough, by taking your box (or folder) of records with you the next time you visit with your accountant or attorney. You can ask your advisor to help you organize your records and assist with your "housecleaning."

Keys are another item to keep up to date. You may have a sentimental reason to keep old keys, but there is no business reason to keep a key to a car you no longer own, a safe deposit box you no longer lease, etc. Keeping such keys can only cause confusion should you become disabled or die. Whoever takes possession of your property will be left with mysterious keys. He will probably think the keys are protecting something of value. Unless you enjoy picturing an heir's frustration as he seeks an imaginary treasure, pitch the key.

Glossary

ABSTRACT OF TITLE An *Abstract of Title* is a condensed history of the title to the land. It consists of a summary of all the documents recorded with the County Recorder that affect the land, including mortgages.

ACTUARIAL TABLE An *actuarial table* is a table organized according to statistical data that indicates the life expectancy of a person.

ADDENDUM An *addendum* to a contract is an addition to the contract.

ADMINISTRATION The *administration* of a Probate Estate is the management and settlement of the decedent's affairs.

ADMINISTRATIVE CODE The *Administrative Code* is the set of rules used by governmental agencies to apply laws enacted by the legislature. The Administrative Code interprets the law and describes the agency's requirements to implement that law. See *CFR*.

ADVANCE MEDICAL DIRECTIVE An *Advance Medical Directive* is a writing made by someone (the *declarant*) in which he gives directions about the health care he wishes to receive in the event he is too ill to speak for himself.

AFFIANT An *Affiant* is someone who signs an affidavit and swears or acknowledges that it is true in the presence of a notary public or other person with authority to administer an oath or take acknowledgments.

AFFIDAVIT An *Affidavit* is a written statement of fact made by someone voluntarily, under oath, or acknowledged as being true, in the presence of a notary public or someone else who has authority to administer an oath or take acknowledgments.

AGENT   An *Agent* is someone who is authorized by another (the principal) to act for or in place of the principal.

AMENDMENT   An *amendment* to a Trust is an addition to the Trust that changes the provisions of the Trust.

ANATOMICAL GIFT   An *anatomical gift* is the donation of all or part of the body of the decedent for a specified purpose, such as transplantation or research.

ANNUAL GIFT TAX EXCLUSION The *Annual Gift Tax Exclusion* is the amount a person can gift to another each year without being required to file a federal Gift Tax Return. The Annual Gift Tax Exclusion is currently $11,000.

ANNUITANT   An *Annuitant* is someone who is entitled to receive payments under an annuity contract.

ANNUITY CONTRACT An *annuity contract* is a contract that gives someone (the annuitant) the right to receive periodic payments (monthly, quarterly) for the life of the annuitant or for a given number of years.

ASSET An *asset* is anything owned by someone that has a value, including personal property (jewelry, paintings, securities, cash, motor vehicles, etc.) and real property (condominiums, vacant lots, acreage, residences, etc.).

ASSIGN To *assign* is to transfer one's rights to another; e.g. a person who has the right to receive income from a partnership may assign that right to another person,

ATTORNEY or ATTORNEY AT LAW An *attorney*, also known as an *Attorney at law*, or a *lawyer*, is someone who is licensed by the state to practice law in that state.

ATTORNEY-IN-FACT An *Attorney-In-Fact* is someone appointed to act as an Agent for another (the Principal) under a Power of Attorney.

AUGMENTED ESTATE In Virginia, the *Augmented Estate* is the value of the decedent's Estate computed for the purpose of determining the surviving spouse's Elective Share.

BASIS The *basis* is a value that is assigned to an asset for the purpose of determining the gain (or loss) on the sale of the item or in determining the value of the item in the hands of someone who has received it as a gift.

BENEFICIARY A *beneficiary* is one who benefits from the act of another or from the transfer of property. In this book we refer to a beneficiary as someone named in a Will, Trust, or deed to receive property, or someone who inherits property under the Laws of Intestate Succession.

BENEFICIARY ACCOUNT A *beneficiary account* is a bank account with a named beneficiary. The owner of the funds in the account directs the bank to give the funds remaining in the account to the named beneficiary upon the death of all of the owners of the bank account. Pay On Death and In Trust For accounts are beneficiary accounts.

BONA FIDE A *bona fide* act is something that is done in good faith; honestly, openly and without deceit or fraud.

CAPITAL GAINS TAX A *Capital Gains Tax* is a tax on the increase in the basis of property sold by a taxpayer.

CASH SURRENDER VALUE The *Cash Surrender Value* of a life insurance policy is the amount of money the insurance company will pay to the owner of an insurance policy in the event the owner cancels the policy before the death of the person who is insured under the policy.

CFR The *Code of Federal Regulations ("CFR")* is the annual cumulation of regulations set by federal executive agencies combined with previous regulations that are still in effect. The CFR contains the general body of laws that govern the practices and procedures of federal administrative agencies.

CHARITABLE REMAINDER ANNUITY TRUST A *Charitable Remainder Annuity Trust* is a Trust that pays an annuity to a designated person (the Annuitant) for a certain period of time or until his death. Once the annuity is paid, whatever remains in the Trust is donated to a tax exempt charity.

CIRCUIT A *circuit* is a judicial division. The state of Virginia is divided into 31 judicial circuits each with its own Circuit Court. Each county has a Circuit Court. Many cities, such as Alexandria, Charlottesville, Fredericksburg, Richmond and Salem have their own Circuit Court.

CLAIM A *claim* against the decedent's Estate is a demand for payment. To be effective, the claim must be filed with the Probate court within the time limits set by law.

CLOSE CORPORATION A *Close Corporation* is a corporation whose voting shares are held by a single shareholder or a small, closely-knit, group of shareholders.

CODE A *Code* is a body of laws arranged systematically for easy reference e.g. the Internal Revenue Code.

CODICIL A *codicil* to a Will is an addition to the Will that changes or replaces certain parts of the Will.

COLUMBARIUM A *columbarium* is a vault with niches (spaces) for urns that contain the ashes of cremated bodies.

COMMON LAW MARRIAGE A *Common Law marriage* is one that is entered into without a state marriage license or any kind of official marriage ceremony. A Common Law marriage is created by an agreement to marry, followed by the two living together, and telling everyone they know that they are husband and wife. Virginia does not recognize a Common Law marriage unless it was entered into in another state that considers the union to be a valid marriage.

COMMUNITY PROPERTY Certain states (Arizona, California, Idaho, Louisiana, Nevada, New Mexico, Texas, Washington, and Wisconsin) have laws stating that property acquired by husband or wife, or both, during their marriage is *Community Property* and is owned equally by both of them.

CONFLICT OF INTEREST A *conflict of interest* is a conflict between the official duties of a fiduciary (guardian, Trustee, attorney, etc.) and his own private interest. For example, it is a conflict of interest for a Successor Trustee to use Trust property for his own personal profit.

CONSERVATOR A *Conservator* is someone appointed by the Probate Court to manage, protect and preserve the property of someone who is missing, or who the Court finds is unable to care for his property because of age (a minor) or incapacity.

CONVENIENCE ACCOUNT A *Convenience Account* is a bank account in which the owner of the funds in the account authorizes another to make bank transactions on his behalf.

CORPORATION A *Corporation* is a company created by one or more persons according to the laws of the state. The company is owned by the *shareholders* or *stockholders*. Each owner has limited liability (see Limited Liability).

COURT The *Court* as used in this book is the Court that handles Probate matters. In Virginia, the Probate Court is a division of the Circuit Court. When referring to an order made by the Court, the term is synonymous with "judge," i.e., an "order of the Court" is an order made by the judge of the Court.

CREDITOR A *creditor* is someone to whom a debt is owed by another person (the *debtor*).

CUSTODIAN A *Custodian* under the *Virginia Uniform Transfers to Minors Act* is a financial institution or person who accepts responsibility for the care and management of property given to a minor child.

DAMAGES *Damages* is money that is awarded by a Court as compensation to someone who has been injured by the action of another.

DEBTOR A *debtor* is someone who owes payment of money or services to another person (the *creditor*).

DECEDENT The *decedent* is the person who died.

DESCENDANT   A *descendant* is someone who descends from a common ancestor. There are two kinds of descendants: a *lineal descendant* and a *collateral descendant*. The lineal descendant is one who descends in a straight line such as father to son to grandson. The collateral descendant is one who descends in a parallel line, such as a cousin. In this book, unless otherwise stated, the term *descendant* refers to a *lineal descendant*. The word *issue* has the same meaning as the word descendant.

DISTRIBUTION The *distribution* of a Trust or Probate Estate is the giving to the beneficiary that part of the Estate to which the beneficiary is entitled.

DURABLE As used in the Power of Attorney, the word *durable* means that the Power of Attorney will remain in effect in the event that the *Principal* (the person giving the Power of Attorney) becomes incapacitated.

ELECTIVE SHARE The *Elective Share* is the minimum amount of the decedent's Estate that a surviving spouse is entitled to receive under law. In Virginia that amount is one third of the decedent's *Augmented Estate*.

ENTITLEMENT An *entitlement* is a legal right to receive a benefit of income, property or services.

EQUITY The *equity* in a home is the market value of the home less monies owed on the property (mortgages, tax liens, etc.)

EQUITY INTEREST   An *equity interest* is an ownership interest. It is the value of the ownership interest over and above monies owed on the property.

ESTATE A person's *Estate* is all of the property (both real and personal property) owned by that person. A person's Estate is also referred to as his *Taxable Estate* because all of the decedent's assets must be included when determining whether any Estate taxes are due when the person dies. Compare to *Probate Estate*.

EXECUTOR   An *Executor* (feminine *Executrix*) is a legal term found in many Wills. The term refers to the person named by the Will maker to carry out directions given in the Will. In modern Wills, that person is referred to as the *Personal Representative*.

FACE VALUE   The *face value* of a life insurance policy is the value stated on the insurance certificate or policy. It is the amount to be paid upon the death of the insured person.

FIDUCIARY A *Fiduciary* is one who takes on the duty of holding property in Trust for another or acting for the benefit of another, such as a Personal Representative, Trustee, Guardian etc.. A fiduciary relationship is also one that is developed out of trust and confidence. For example, an attorney has a fiduciary relationship with his client.

GRANTEE   The *Grantee* of a deed is the person who receives title to real property from the *Grantor*.

GRANTOR The *Grantor* is someone who transfers property. The Grantor of a deed, is the person who transfers real property to a new owner (the Grantee). The Grantor of a Trust is someone who creates the Trust and then transfers property into the Trust. Also see *Settlor*.

GUARANTOR A *Guarantor* is someone who promises to pay a debt or perform a contract for another in the event that person does not fulfill his obligation.

GUARDIAN   A *Guardian* is someone who has legal authority to care for the person or property of a minor or for someone who has been found by the court to be incapacitated.

GUARDIAN AD LITEM   A *Guardian Ad Litem* is a special Guardian appointed by the Court to represent the interests of a minor, or someone who is incapacitated, during a Court proceeding.

HEALTH CARE AGENT   A *Health Care Agent* is someone who is appointed by another (the *Principal)* to authorize medical treatment for the Principal, in the event the Principal is to too ill to do so himself.

HEIR   An *Heir* is anyone entitled to inherit the decedent's property under the Laws of Descent in the event that the decedent dies without a valid Will.

HOLOGRAPHIC WILL A *Holographic Will* is a Will written, dated and signed by the hand of the Will maker himself. Many states refuse to admit a Holographic Will into Probate unless it is witnessed according to the laws of the state.

HOMESTEAD The *homestead* is the dwelling that is owned, and occupied, in the Commonwealth of Virginia as the owner's principal residence.

INCAPACITATED   The term *incapacitated* is used in two ways. A person is *physically incapacitated* if he lacks the ability to perform certain tasks. A person is *legally incapacitated* if a Court finds that he is unable to care for his person or property.

INTER VIVOS TRUST   An *Inter Vivos Trust* (also known as a *Living Trust*) is a Trust that is created and becomes effective during the lifetime of the Settlor (or Grantor) as contrasted with a Trust that the Settlor includes as part of his Will to take effect upon his death.

IRREVOCABLE CONTRACT An *irrevocable contract* is a contract that cannot be revoked, withdrawn, or cancelled by any of the parties to that contract.

IRREVOCABLE TRUST An *Irrevocable Trust* is a Trust that cannot be cancelled or terminated until its purpose is accomplished.

IRREVOCABLE INSURANCE TRUST   An *Irrevocable Insurance Trust* is a Trust that is set up to purchase life insurance. The proceeds of the life insurance policy can be used to pay taxes that may be due upon the death of the insured person.

IRA ACCOUNT An *Individual Retirement Account ("IRA")* is a retirement savings account in which income taxes on certain deposits and interest to the account are deferred until the monies are withdrawn from the account.

JOINT AND SEVERAL LIABILITY If two or more people agree to be *jointly and severally liable* to pay a debt, then each individually agrees to be responsible to pay the debt, and together they all agree to pay for the debt.

KEOGH PLAN   A *Keogh Plan* is a retirement plan available to self-employed taxpayers. Certain tax benefits are available such as tax deductions for annual contributions to the plan. The plan is named for its author, Eugene James Keogh.

KEY MAN INSURANCE *Key man insurance* is a disability and life insurance policy designed to protect a company from economic loss in the event that an important employee of the company becomes disabled or dies.

LAWS OF DESCENT AND DISTRIBUTION The *Laws of Descent and Distribution* (also known as the *Laws of Intestate Succession*) are the laws of the state that determine who is to inherit the decedent's Probate Estate if the decedent died without a valid Will.

LEGALESE *Legalese* refers to the use of legal terms and confusing text used by some attorneys when drafting legal documents.

LIEN A *lien* is a charge against a person's property as security for a debt. The lien is evidence of the creditor's right to take the property as full or partial payment, in the event that the debtor defaults in paying the monies owed.

LIFE ESTATE A *Life Estate* interest in real property is the right to possess and receive the income from that property for so long as the holder of the Life Estate lives. A one-third Life Estate interest means the person can occupy one-third of the property or receive one-third of the income generated by that property.

LIMITED LIABILITY *Limited Liability,* as related to a corporation or other company created according to state law, means that a shareholder of the company generally is not responsible to pay the debts of the company beyond the amount that he/she invested in the company.

LIMITED LIABILITY COMPANY A *Limited Liability Company* is a company created according to the laws of the state. In Virginia, it can be organized to conduct any lawful business. All of the members of the company have limited liability.

LIMITED PARTNERSHIP A *Limited Partnership* is a partnership created according to the laws of the state. Each *Limited Partner* has limited liability. Each *General Partner* has control of the business and is personally liable for all of the debts of the company. (See Limited Liability).

LINEAL DESCENDANT See *descendant.*

LITIGATION *Litigation* is the process of carrying on a lawsuit, i.e., to sue for some right or remedy in a court of law. A Litigation Attorney is one who is experienced in conducting the law suit and in particular, going to trial.

LIVING WILL A *Living Will* is a Health Care Directive that gives instructions to the physician about whether life support systems should be withheld or withdrawn in the event that the person who signs the Living Will is terminally ill or in a persistent vegetative state and unable to speak for himself.

LOOK-BACK PERIOD The *Look-back Period* is a period of consecutive months that can be reviewed for transfers of Resources to determine whether a period of ineligibility should be imposed for the Medicaid Applicant.

MEDICAID *Medicaid* is a medical assistance program sponsored jointly by the federal and state government to provide health care for people with low income and limited resources. In Virginia, the program is also referred to as *Medical Assistance.*

NET WORTH A person's *net worth* is the value of all of the property that he owns less what he owes.

NEXT OF KIN *Next of kin* has two meanings in law: *next of kin* refers to a person's nearest blood relation or it can refer to those people (not necessarily blood relations) who are entitled to inherit the property of a person who dies without a valid Will.

NON-PROBATE TRANSFER A *Non-Probate Transfer* is a transfer made to a beneficiary of the decedent without going through a Probate procedure. This includes transfers from a joint account, a Trust, a Pay-On-Death account, a Transfer-On-Death security, etc.

PARTNERSHIP A business *partnership* is an agreement between two or more persons to use their assets and/or services to carry on a business for profit as co-owners.

PERSONAL EFFECTS *Personal effects* is personal property that is kept for one's personal use such as clothing, jewelry, books, and other items generally found in the home.

PERSONAL PROPERTY *Personal property* is all property owned by a person that is not real property (real estate). It includes personal effects, cars, securities, bank accounts, insurance policies, etc.

PERSONAL REPRESENTATIVE   The *Personal Representative* is someone appointed by the Probate Court to settle the decedent's Estate and to distribute whatever is left to the proper beneficiary.

PER STIRPES *Per Stirpes* is a method of distributing property to a group of beneficiaries in the event that one of them dies before the gift is made. The deceased person's share goes to his descendants, and if none, the surviving beneficiaries share equally in the gift.

PETITION A *Petition* is a formal written, request to a Court asking the Court to take action or issue an order on a given matter; e.g. a request to appoint a Guardian.

POSTNUPTIAL AGREEMENT A *Postnuptial Agreement* is an Agreement made by a couple after marriage to decide their respective rights in the event of a dissolution or the death of a spouse.

POWER OF ATTORNEY A *Power of Attorney* is a document in which someone (the *Principal*) gives another (his *Agent*) authority to do specific things on behalf of the Principal.

PRENUPTIAL AGREEMENT A *Prenuptial Agreement* (also known as an *Antenuptial Agreement*) is an agreement made prior to marriage whereby a couple determines how their property is to be managed during their marriage and how their property is to be divided should either die, or they later divorce.

PRINCIPAL OF A POWER OF ATTORNEY The *Principal* of a Power of Attorney is someone who gives another (his *Agent*) authority to act on his (the Principal's) behalf.

PRINCIPAL OF A TRUST The *Principal* of a Trust is the Trust property. The Trust income are the monies that are earned on the Trust Principal.

PROBABLE CAUSE   *Probable cause* exists if it is reasonable to believe certain facts. Mere suspicion is not enough. For probable cause to exist, there must be more evidence for the facts than against.

PROBATE   *Probate* is a Court procedure in which a Court determines the existence of a valid Will. The Decedent's Estate is settled by the Personal Representative who pays all valid claims and then distributes whatever remains to the proper beneficiary.

PROBATE ESTATE The *Probate Estate* is that part of the decedent's Estate that is subject to a Probate procedure. It includes property that the decedent owned in his name only. It does not include property that was jointly held by the decedent and someone else. It does not include property held "in trust for" or "for the benefit of" someone.

PRO BONO The term *Pro Bono* means "for the public good." When an attorney works Pro Bono, he does so voluntarily and without pay.

REAL PROPERTY *Real property*, also known as *real estate,* is land and anything permanently attached to the land such as buildings and fences.

REMAINDER INTEREST   A *Remainder Interest* in real property is the property that passes to a beneficiary at the end of the life interest i.e. the property that passes to the beneficiary once the owner of the Life Estate dies.

RESIDUARY BENEFICIARY A *residuary beneficiary* of a Will is a beneficiary who is entitled to whatever is left of the Probate Estate once the specific gifts made in the Will have been distributed and once the decedent's bills, taxes and costs of Probate have been paid. If there is more than one residuary beneficiary, then unless the Will provides differently, they all share equally in the residuary Estate.

RESOURCE A *Resource* for purposes of determining Medicaid eligibility, is an asset owned by the decedent, or his spouse, that can be converted to meet their needs. Federal statute 42 U.S.C. 1382b identifies what is (and is not) counted as a Resource.

REVOCABLE TRUST A *Revocable Trust* is a Trust that can be amended or revoked by the Grantor or Settlor during his lifetime.

REVOCABLE LIVING TRUST A *Revocable Living Trust* (also known as an *Inter Vivos Trust*) is a Revocable Trust that is created and becomes effective during the lifetime of the Grantor or Settlor.

SETTLOR A *Settlor* or a *Trustor* is someone who creates a Trust.

SIBLING   A *sibling* is one of two or more people born of the same parents; i.e., a brother or a sister. Unless, otherwise noted, we used the term to include those who have only one parent in common; i.e. a half brother or a half sister.

SOLE PROPRIETORSHIP   A *Sole Proprietorship* is a form of business ownership in which one person owns all of the assets of the business and that person is personally liable for all of the debts of the business.

SOLEMNIZE   To *solemnize* a marriage is to enter into the marriage publicly, before witnesses, in contrast to a secretive or common law marriage.

SPECIFIC GIFT   A *Specific Gift* is a gift of a specific item of the Will maker's Estate that is made to a named beneficiary of the Will.

SPENDTHRIFT   A *Spendthrift* is someone who wastes money and/or spends lavishly.

SPENDTHRIFT TRUST   A *Spendthrift Trust* is a Trust created to provide monies for the living expenses of a beneficiary, and at the same time protect the monies from being taken by the creditors of the beneficiary.

SPRINGING POWER OF ATTORNEY   A *Springing Power of Attorney* is a Power of Attorney that is not operational until, and unless, the Principal is incapacitated.

STANDBY GUARDIAN   A *Standby Guardian* is someone appointed by a parent to take over the care of a child in the event that the parent becomes incapacitated or dies.

STATUTE OF LIMITATION A *Statute of Limitation* is a federal or state law that sets maximum time periods for taking legal action. Once the time set out in the statute passes, no legal action can be taken.

STEPPED-UP BASIS A *stepped-up basis* is the value placed on property that is acquired in a taxable transaction such as inheriting property or purchasing property (Internal Revenue Code 1012). The "step-up" refers to the increase in value from the basis of the former owner (usually what he paid for it), to the basis of the new owner (usually the market value when the transfer is made).

SUCCESSOR TRUSTEE   A *Successor Trustee* is someone who takes the place of the Trustee.

SURROGATE A *Surrogate* is a substitute; someone who acts in place of another.

TENANCY BY THE ENTIRETY A *Tenancy by the Entirety* is the name of a form of ownership of real property held by a husband and wife. It is a joint tenancy with right of survivorship, modified by the common law theory that the husband and wife are one. With a joint tenancy with right of survivor, each joint tenant owns their own share of the property until death, when the surviving owner owns it 100%. With a Tenancy by the Entirety, each owns 100% of the property both before and after death.

TENANCY IN COMMON   *Tenancy In Common* is a form of ownership such that each tenant owns his share without any claim to that share by the other tenants. Unlike a joint tenancy, there is no Right of Survivorship. Once a Tenant In Common dies, his share becomes part of his Estate.

TERM LIFE INSURANCE POLICY   A *Term Life Insurance policy* insures the life of a person for a certain period of time. No insurance proceeds are paid unless the insured person dies within the given period of time. The monies paid for the policy are not refundable, so a Term Life Insurance policy has no cash surrender value.

TITLE INSURANCE *Title Insurance* is a policy issued by a title insurance company after searching title to the property. The insurance covers losses that result from a defect of title, such as unpaid taxes, or someone has ap claim of ownership of the property.

TRUST AGREEMENT A *Trust agreement* is a document in which someone (the Grantor or Settlor) creates a Trust and appoints a Trustee to manage property placed into the Trust. The usual purpose of the Trust is to benefit persons or charities named by the Grantor as beneficiaries of the Trust.

TRUSTEE   A *Trustee* is a person, or institution, who accepts the duty of caring for property for the benefit of another.

UNASSIGNABLE ANNUITY   An *unassignable annuity* is an annuity that cannot be assigned; i.e., the annuitant's benefits cannot be transferred to another.

UNDUE INFLUENCE   *Undue influence* is pressure, influence or persuasion that overpowers a person's free will or judgment, so that a person acts according to the will or purpose of the dominating party.

UNSECURED CREDITOR An *unsecured creditor* is someone who is owed money on a promissory note with nothing to back it up if payment is not made. A *secured creditor* holds some special assurance of payment, such as a mortgage on real property or a lien on a car.

VAC   *VAC* is the abbreviation for the Virginia Administrative Code.

VDSS The *Virginia Department of Social Services ("VDSS)* is the state agency that administers Virginia's Medical Assistance program.

VOID PROVISION   A *void provision* is one that is not legally enforceable. For example, if a Will provision makes a gift and the Court finds that provision to be void, then the beneficiary has no legal right to receive that gift.

WAIVER   A *waiver* is the intentional and voluntary giving up of a known right.

WARRANTY DEED   A ***Warranty Deed*** is a deed in which the Grantor warrants (promises) that the property he is transferring has good and clear title; i.e., that no one else has rights in the property. This is different than a ***Quit-claim Deed*** where the Grantor says, in effect, "I am releasing any interest I have in this property to you, but I make no guarantees about anyone else's right to this property."

WAIVER   A *waiver* is the intentional and voluntary giving up of a known right.

WARD   A ***Ward*** is a minor or an incapacitated person who is placed by the Court under the care and supervision of a Guardian or a Conservator.

INDEX

A Will Is Not Enough In Virginia

Each state has its own set of laws relating to the control, and protection of a person's Estate. The laws of Virginia relating to Guardianship, Probate and especially Medicaid are very different from the laws of other states.

The author is in the process of "translating" *A Will Is Not Enough* for the rest of the states; that is, writing state specific books that explain how to set up an Estate Plan for the given state and how to qualify for MEDICAID in that state.

A Will Is Not Enough is now available for:
ARIZONA, CALIFORNIA, CONNECTICUT, COLORADO
FLORIDA, HAWAII, INDIANA, MARYLAND
MICHIGAN, MASSACHUSETTS, NEBRASKA
NEW JERSEY, NEW MEXICO, NEW YORK,
OREGON, PENNSYLVANIA, TEXAS
VIRGINIA, WASHINGTON, WISCONSIN.

To check whether this book is currently available for other states call Eagle Publishing Company of Boca at
(800) 824-0823
or visit our Web site http://www.eaglepublishing.com

SPECIAL OFFER FOR PURCHASERS OF THIS BOOK
$25 INCLUDES SHIPPING

How To Defend Yourself Against Your Lawyer

is a book about the unhappy experiences people have with their lawyers, beginning with that of the author AMELIA E. POHL. She became involved in a law suit and found herself in the role of client, rather than lawyer. She become concerned about lawyers who do not provide their clients with the loyalty and respect due to them. This book is a result of those concerns.

The book is divided into chapters that cover the most common problems that take people to a lawyer: divorce, probate, criminal, personal injury, starting a business, making a Will, buying a house, etc. Each chapter tells of the misadventures of the unwary as they sought the services of a lawyer without a clue as to what they were "buying." This book is funny, sad, interesting, but most of all informative. It tells the reader how to become a savvy consumer, i.e., how to find the right lawyer for the right job. If the reader ever finds the need to employ a lawyer, he will be glad he read this book.

Copyright 2004   272 pages 6" X 9" soft cover
$20 includes Shipping and Handling

Beyond Grief To Acceptance and Peace

AMELIA E. POHL and the noted psychologist BARBARA J. SIMMONDS, Ph.d, have written a book for those families who have suffered a loss.

What to say to the bereaved
- ✧ How to help a child through the loss
- ✧ Strategies to adjust to a new life-style
- ✧ When and where to seek assistance.

80 pages   6" X 9" $10 includes Shipping and Handling

Guiding Those Left Behind

Amelia E. Pohl has written a series of books explaining how to settle an Estate. Each book is state specific, telling how things are done in that state. Each book explains:

✧ who to notify
✧ how to locate the decedent's property
✧ how to get possession of the inheritance
✧ when you do, and do not, need an attorney
✧ the rights of a beneficiary, and much more.

Each book is written with the assistance of an experienced attorney who is licensed and is practicing in that state.

The *Guiding* series is currently available for the following states: ALABAMA, ARIZONA, CALIFORNIA, CONNECTICUT
FLORIDA, GEORGIA, HAWAII, ILLINOIS, INDIANA
IOWA, KENTUCKY, LOUISIANA, MASSACHUSETTS
MARYLAND, MICHIGAN, MINNESOTA, MISSOURI
MISSISSIPPI, NEW JERSEY, NEW YORK
NORTH CAROLINA, OHIO, OKLAHOMA
PENNSYLVANIA, SOUTH CAROLINA, TENNESSEE
TEXAS, VIRGINIA, WASHINGTON, WISCONSIN

Visit our Web site http://www.eaglepublishing.com
to check whether books for other states are available at this time.

SPECIAL OFFER FOR PURCHASERS OF THIS BOOK
$22 INCLUDES SHIPPING

To order call (800) 824-0823

It is the goal of EAGLE PUBLISHING COMPANY to keep our publications fresh.

As we receive information about changes to the federal or Virginia law we will post an update to this edition at our Web site:

http://www.eaglepublishing.com